The Torrey Pines Murders

Pete Driscoll

Published by Trellis Publishing, 2021.

THE TORREY PINES MURDERS

First edition. July 4, 2021.

Copyright © 2021 Pete Driscoll.

ISBN: 979-8224884094

Written by Pete Driscoll.

THE TORREY PINES MURDERS

PETE DRISCOLL

1

The Torrey Pines beach killings are two of the most hideous, savage murders in California history, made seemingly worse by the beautiful location at which they took place. But, as time has failed to heal the wounds torn into families by these horrific events, it now seems as though the crimes that took place could have claimed a third, and maybe even a fourth, victim.

By day, the beautiful, stunning beach in San Diego, Southern California is a hot spot for sun seekers, surfers and those looking for a walk by the sea. The glittering ocean is contained, it appears, within the magnificent nearby cliffs and the long, wide soft sandy beach sneaks slowly towards an esplanade, complete with inevitable parking lot. The arches of a wide bridge provide a touch of privacy and quiet. Life towers offer safety from the waves.

As wonderful as Torrey Pines is during the day, at night it changes. The dark brings out shadows. And those shadows became a lot deeper after the night of August 12th, 1978.

Barbara Natais was fifteen. Barbara was a live wire, the life and soul of the party. She was an independently minded girl, keen to test the boundaries of her world, like most fifteen-year-old kids. She had grown up local to San Diego, and knew of the attractions of Torrey Pines.

Her mother, Julie, said of her daughter: 'She was a popular, defiant, beautiful pain in the arse. God gave to me to keep my humble.' Dad, Ralph, admired her independence 'She was as tough as nails,' he lamented.

Also in the family were sisters Lorraine and Sue. Like many siblings, Sue and Barbara did not always get on. 'She was outspoken, stubborn and set in her ways. We had lots of arguments,' remembered Sue. But for all that, they were a close and loving family.

Barbara was in a stable, long term relationship with Jim Alt, a slightly older boy. His long, flowing blond locks, well-tuned and slim body and fondness for the surf made him a pin up, and idol of teenage girls. Indeed, he had recently appeared on the cover of a local surfing publication. His close friend Rick Selga said of his fellow board enthusiast: 'He was a big, strong, funny, happy guy. He was probably the guy everybody looked up to,'

During that fateful Summer, Ralph and Julie planned on a couple of nights away. They left Sue in charge, and perhaps in a premonition that something was about to go wrong, Ralph took Jim aside, and told him to 'look after' his daughter.

It was a task Jim could not complete, and something that it took a long time for Ralph to forgive. In the grief of the aftermath, he needed somebody to blame, and in the absence of an obvious suspect, that anger turned towards his daughter's boyfriend. It would be years later that Ralph came to terms with the fact that Jim was not to blame for failing to protect his little girl.

As soon as the parents had loaded their car and left, Jim and Rick, Barbara and Rick's own girlfriend jumped into a station wagon and headed for the beach, even though Jim had promised his girlfriend's father that they would stay put while her parents were away.

'It was the biggest mistake of my life' Jim still reflects nearly forty years on.

The four friends ended up at the beach. It was packed, the parking lot full of cars. The atmosphere was like a party.

Around 9pm the beach began to clear, and the fun was over. Jim and Barbara grabbed their sleeping bags and headed once more for the sand. They zipped the sleeping bags together, and fell asleep in each other's arms. Meanwhile, Jim and his girlfriend slept in the station wagon. Both couples wanted a touch of privacy.

Jim woke the next morning and found he was covered in blood. He could not see anything and feared he had been blinded. He felt his way up the hill to the parking lot. He rapped on the window of the station wagon from low down on the floor. He was not able to get to his feet.

'His face was swollen, blood all over his blond hair,' said Rick, describing his friend, whose head was blown up with the swellings from his wounds.

He had been attacked with a rock and a log from a fire pit from the beach. Regaining a little of his strength, Jim staggered down beach looking for Barbara. He soon found her, nude and dead.

Paul Ybarrondo was a sergeant with the local police department in San Diego. He was one of the first officers on the scene.

'She had some severe looking wounds on her head,' he said. She also had sand in her mouth. Somebody had taken a sharp instrument and cut around the nipple of her breast. She had been raped and sodomised. The viciousness of the attack was a shock to even the hardened officers of the San Diego police department. Next, they had the unpleasant task of informing Barbara's parents of their gruesome discovery. Ralph and Julie did not even know that Barbara had gone out. They thought that she would be at home with her sisters.

'It was like somebody took a sledge hammer to my head. We didn't even know that she was down there' said her father, recalling the delivery of the dreadful news.

Meanwhile Jim was rushed to the hospital. He was in a coma for days, and when he awoke he had no memory of the attack. His head is still filled with steel. He was quickly ruled out as a suspect. Even today, so many years later, the memories of that night come back to haunt him.

'I put my hands on the bed, and I feel for that sheet, or I feel for sand on the beach,' he said on the CBS True Crime Documentary programme, '48 Hours', which ran a special on the Torrey Pines murders in 2016. 'She has brown hair, brown eyes. I love her.' The presence of his boyhood girlfriend is still present in Jim Alt's mind.

A $2000 reward was offered, but no leads came about. The case slowly went cold, and drifted out of the public's imagination, until, that was, six years later, in the Summer of 1984 when a beachcomber made a discovery he would have preferred to have avoided.

Clair Hough was intelligent girl, only 14 but mature for her age. She was very much her own person, and would eschew the traditional past times of teenage girls to go for walks with her friends on the seashore. She adored the beach. Kim Jamer was her best friend, and was often her companion on those walks by the sea. She described Clair as spirited and independent. 'She just had an inner life, a joy about her.'

Clair was funny, gentle and kind. She was the class mediator, and would not put up with injustice, even if it got her in trouble at school.

She grew up on Rhode Island and loved to patrol the beach with Kim. She would take her mother home things she found in the sea, pretty treasures that she gave as keepsakes. Her grandparents lived a short distance from Torrey Pines beach. In 1984 the parents sent Clair and her brother, along with Kim Jamer, off to California to stay with Clair's grandparents.

It was liberating to the teenagers, who could be silly and girlish without anybody knowing who they were. On the final night of Kim's stay, Clair persuaded Kim to sneak out, and go to the beach late.

They settled by the bridge, initially enjoying the dark and the quiet, until Kim had a panic attack. She made her friend promise that she would not sneak out after dark – the beach was vulnerable at night.

Kim stated on '48 Hours' that she had told her friend not to go down to the beach at night by herself. 'Do not go down there alone,' Kim advised, but her friend was headstrong, and did not listen. It is something that haunts her friend still, over thirty years later. 'She was my best friend. I think about her every day'

Kim headed home to Rhode Island, but Clair broke her promise.

On August 24th 1984 a beachcomber found Clair's body on the beach. Paul Ybarronda also worked on her case.

At the time of her discovery, the officer saw many similarities between the two crimes which had been committed within two life towers of each other. Like Barbara, Clair too was sexually assaulted, and also had sand thrust deep in her mouth. Tellingly, she also had her breast mutilated. Her autopsy report noted, with the coldness of officialdom and formality: 'Right breast, linear abrasions'

The first suspect soon emerged. Wallace Wheeler was the beachcomber who found the young girl's body. He claimed to be a psychic.

The police encouraged the Hough's to keep in touch with Wheeler. They had their suspicions about the man, and hoped that he might either confess or at least let something slip.

He would write lengthy, rambling letters to the Houghs stating that Clair was coming to him in visions. He described her 'smiling' face and told her grieving parents that 'her eyes were radiant.'

The letters were peculiar, and a cause of alarm to the police. But Wheeler did not confess to any crime. Eventually the letters stopped. The reason was that Wheeler, a former Lieutenant in the US Air Corps, who had fought in World War two, was dead. He was in his 60s when he leapt from a block of flats, plummeting to the ground in his suicidal leap.

Back in Rhode Island, the Houghs were desperate for any lead the police might gain. Grief hits in mysterious ways. For Clair's mother, it came in the form of guilt. 'I felt I was a failure as a mother,' she said. Once more, progress on the case halted, and public interest in the murders began to fade. But for two sets of families, the horror continued.

The Houghs believed that Wheeler was the killer. But the Nantais had never heard of the beachcomber. The two sets of still grieving parents also knew nothing pef the possibility that their daughters had been the victim of a serial killer.

It was in 2008 that the San Diego police Department listed the cases on its website. For the first time, the authorities accepted that it was in all probability the same killer who had murdered both girls.

Barbara's sister was furious, along with the families, that they had never been informed of the probably link.

But there would still be no immediate break through. Then, in 2012, advances in DNA testing brought two suspects to the attention of police. And one of these was a man who had worked closely with the force.

Blood on Clair's jeans linked her to a convicted rapist, Ronald Catro. And a tiny amount of DNA, discovered internally in Clair, suggested Kevin Brown, a former criminalist who had worked in the San Diego's police laboratory.

Rebecca Brown had been married to Kevin for more than twenty years. They had met via the classified ads, how it used to be in the old days before online dating. Rebecca was immediately impressed with her blind date. Kevin Brown was an old-style gentleman, the type who held open car doors. He shared her love of animals as well. Soon they were married. The Browns' life was quiet; they liked to travel, they kept pets and they were regular and committed church goers.

Then, in January of 2014, police investigators visited Rebecca's home. She first thought that they had come to discuss some old case on which her husband had worked. But soon she learned news that would turn both of their lives upside down.

The police showed a picture of Ronald Clyde Tatro to Kevin Brown, and asked if he knew the man. He denied any knowledge of the convicted rapist. However, the police were unable to cross check with Tatro himself. He had drowned in what had been concluded as a boating accident in Tennessee in 2011. Although, suspicion remained that it was suicide that had killed the convicted felon. His wallet and glasses had been placed neatly on the seat of his rowing boat, and the day of his death was the anniversary of the murder of Clair Hough.

That left Kevin Brown as the only living suspect. When police informed him that his DNA had been found on the body, it was Kevin who suggested it might have come from a vaginal swab. Police immediately organised a search warrant for the property, seeking out mementoes or other links to the 30-year-old crimes. They found nothing.

Rebecca remains convinced that her husband was not capable of killing anybody, but investigators held a different opinion. They knew that Kevin Brown had another side to his character, different to the one that his wife saw daily.

At the time of Clair Hough's death, he was a bachelor in his thirties and had a reputation at the crime lab, one gained from his fondness for attending strip clubs. 'Kinky' was the name by which he was known by his colleagues.

He also enjoyed going to see pornographic movies with friends. While there was nothing more than this that his male colleagues knew about for sure, female workers at the lab sometimes saw a different side to Brown. Once, a female co-worker, reported Brown to their bosses. She claimed that he had read aloud to her a report of a particularly violent rape, referring to it, she reported, as 'funny'. It disconcerted the colleague so much that she did her best to avoid working with him in the future. .

He also enjoyed photography, and would get involved in 'lingerie' shots. Rocky Ferguson was a fellow photographer, and he knew that some picture takers would arrange private, racier sessions.

When asked if he knew the second young victim of the Torrey Pines murders, he initially denied any knowledge of knowing Clair Hough. Later, though, Kevin went back to police and told them that now he could recall somebody named Clair; he did not know her last name but recalled having sex with her at some point in the early 1980s.

But to Kevin's wife, such evidence was freely given and not indicative of any crime having been committed. 'I never thought he was a killer. Never, Never. He didn't have a mean bone in his body,' she said.

Rebecca was unconcerned too about his photography sessions. 'He had a normal, male sex drive.' she said, 'and he was single back in those days.' There was nothing untoward about his behaviour, she believed.

The Browns' attorneys too saw major differences between the killings, violent and sadistic as they were, and Kevin Brown's propensity for enjoying taking some racy, adult photographs.

There was also no evidence that Brown knew the convicted rapist, Ron Tatro

There was no evidence, however, that the 'Clair' Brown had met was Clair Hough. The woman he described was much older, in her thirties. Although it confused the case, Brown's attorneys believe that their man had been persecuted for simply being honest.

Richard Von Helm, the attorney, believe that the detectives had decided early on that Brown was guilty, and therefore skewed everything the former criminologist said to make him appear as the killer.

In fact, they had little hard evidence. Police relied heavily on an alleged statement that Brown spoke to a friend, saying he had photographed a 'girl' on the beach, and now he discovered that she had been murdered. Richard Von Helm disputes that this is what Brown's friend said.

Brown's performance when questioned by police did not help his case. Even his former colleagues at the criminology department said that Brown was always nervous under pressure. He would have appeared jittery when questioned, something that might lead police to believe he had something to hide.

He did not have a good record when working for the police and supporting cases in court. That was simply Kevin Brown's character. A quiet man, not a killer nervous about the truth.

Von Helm also casts doubt on the DNA evidence. Firstly, there were several swabs taken from inside Clair Hough's vagina and not all of these contained any evidence of DNA from Kevin Brown. The one swab that did, the attorney insists, had been compromised by the way it had been kept. Back in the early and mid-1980s, techniques for storing DNA were weak, and evidence was frequently contaminated.

Although Brown was not involved in the original Clair Hough investigation, he was close to the criminologist looking after the case. Astonishingly, from today's perspective, the swab in question was laid to dry, uncapped, in the open air on a table close to where Kevin Brown worked. Cross contamination was not only possible, but likely. Many cases relying on developments in DNA identification had fallen down because of this. And not only in California, but across the entire country as well.

The DNA evidence found on the swab was, though, semen, and it is hard to see how that fluid could find its way into Clair Hough's vagina unless it was deposited during rape, Nevertheless, a probable scenario was soon identified by the attorneys and Kevin's friends from his criminology days. Back in the 1980s, the chemicals used for detecting DNA had to be checked, and one of the ways that criminologists would do this was to use their own bodily fluids to carry out tests. Blood, sweat, saliva and even seminal fluids were present in the working environment, and could easily contaminate an unprotected swab.

A former criminologist who worked closely with Kevin Brown at the San Diego Police Department was able to offer a clear possibility of how the cross contamination might occur. 'We didn't change gloves in those days. It is possible that the criminologist testing the case used Kevin's semen to test the chemicals, and then wore the same gloves to work on the swab. I believe that they lacked the evidence necessary to charge Mr Kevin Brown with these murders,' he concluded.

Then, on October 20th 2014 events took a further, macabre turn. Rebecca found Kevin's bible sitting on the table and he had underlined a psalm which talks about being wrongfully accused.

He had left behind his watch and his cell phone, and had told his mother in law that he had to go out, that he had 'things to do.'

He did not return that evening, and the next day, a knock on the door revealed a couple of policeman. They told Rebecca that they had found her husband.

The Browns had a vacation cabin in a park, and a ranger had found the body of Kevin. It was hanging from a tree.

'I totally understand why people might think that he didn't want to go court, where he could clear his name. Some would never believe it. It would tarnish his name. He was so proud of it,' said Rebecca tearfully on the '48 Hours' documentary.

Shortly after the discovery of Kevin Brown's body, police launched a press conference in which they announced that they had two suspects for the Torrey Pines murders. Both were now dead, and one of these was Kevin Brown.

A police spokesman said 'We have a very strong case to name Ron Treto and Kevin Brown as suspects in…these cases. An arrest of Kevin Brown would have been forthcoming.'

This makes Kevin's wife bitterly angry. There was never enough evidence to arrest him during his lifetime, when he would have been there to answer any charges. There certainly was not enough to convict him after his death. 'Now that he's gone you (the police) are just going to say: "You did it. Case solved. All done,"' she raged.

Rebecca decided not to take what she saw as the persecution of her husband lying down. She herself has filed civil charges against two San Diego police officers for misconduct and wrongful death.

But Clair Hough's parents, Penny and Sam, take a different view. They are confident in the San Diego police department, happy with their findings. Now, the details around the death of their daughter is less important than remembering her life. They have come to terms with her demise, and now want to celebrate her life.

Clair Hough was a young girl with foresight. She even left a will, despite her tender age. It is something that is particularly important now to the couple. Written in the document are the words:

'You made me realise how precious and beautiful life is. Thank you.' And later, 'I wish I could list all the wonderful things you've done, but everyone would fall asleep. I love you both.' That the words are written in a young, immature hand adds to the tragedy of it all.

If the Houghs have, as far as will ever be possible, come to terms with the death of their daughter, the same cannot be said of the Rantais. They retain a sense of confusion over the entire event. 'I want to know her. I want her to have a life,' weeps her mother.

And to police, it now seems as though the cases are not connected. The links between them, once regarded as so concrete, are now viewed as just coincidental. A key reason for this is that Ronald Tatro and Kevin Brown each had a perfect, indisputable alibi for their whereabouts at the time of the murder of Barbara. Tatro was in prison, while Brown was at college, five hundred miles away in Sacramento.

If the two are, as is the case in the eyes of the police, somehow responsible for Clair's murder, then there is no way that the two crimes could be connected. To Jim Alt, the police's position is unsatisfactory. 'We want answers. We want to know what the police are doing about this,' he said. His own guilt lies, on his own admission, partially behind his anger. He explained: 'Because of a decision Barbara and I made, she never came home.'

Officially, the case of Barbara Rantais remains open, while police consider the crime against Clair Hough as closed. But such a conclusion remains one that fails to satisfy many of those closest to the case. The similarities between the murders of Barbara Rantais and Clair Hough are too great to suggest coincidence. Unless the second killing was a copycat of the first, then to attack two teenaged girls, late at night on the same beach, close to the same spot is too suggestive of the same killer to ignore. Add to that the fact that both girls were sexually assaulted, violently and without any evidence of pity and the likelihood that the perpetrator is the same man increases. That probability is enhanced further when it is known that both victims endured the unusual and sadistic mutilation of one breast.

To suggest that murders were carried out by different people allows the police to leave the blame for Clair's killing soundly at the door of Kevin Brown. But evidence is circumstantial at best. While he might have enjoyed, before his marriage, a seedy interest in porn and in photographing willing women in 'adult' poses, such actions are not a crime provided all involved are consenting adults. Further, his character seems out of synch with somebody who could virtually cut off the breast of a young girl, as well as rape and murder her. And such evidence as does exist against him is highly questionable.

The strongest signs suggesting that the crimes were committed by different people lies in the involvement, if any, of Ronald Tatro. It was impossible for him to have been present at the death of Barbara because he was incarcerated at the time. But DNA evidence suggests his blood was found on Clair's jeans. However, we know that police procedures in the 1980s were not as professional as today. We know that the care taken with preserving the integrity of DNA evidence was not as thorough back then. We also know that political pressures to solve a crime was more likely to carry weight.

Torrey Pines is a tourist spot, a place of great beauty that generates much trade form locals and visitors. For that place to become associated with murder, particularly of children, impacted enormously on its attraction. Such an outcome was inevitable. Who can tell if the police, at some level, were put under pressure, or felt the need, to find a quick solution to their problem? We are unlikely to discover now whether this was indeed a factor.

But what we can say regarding the entire thirty-six-year history of the Torrey Pines murders is that they are still victims, still people suffering. Ronald Tetro may not be widely missed. His death may have been, as was recorded, a simple boating accident, even though there is circumstantial evidence suggesting otherwise. His death on the anniversary of the murder of Clair Hough might be coincidence. Then again it might not. But if Tetro is a victim of Torrey Pines, then his passing will be unregretted by all but his closest family. The second and third, definite, victims of the farrago are Barbara Rantais and Clair Hough, and their families continue to suffer daily. That is even though the Houghs have attempted to move on with their lives, to celebrate their daughter rather than mourn her.

The family and friends of Kevin Brown, and the man himself, are the final set of people to suffer as a result of crimes committed on that stretch of beautiful landscape in San Diego. They remain convinced that Kevin was not involved in the death of Clair Hough, and that his own demise, his suicide, was a direct result of the persecution he felt at the hands of the local police. Whether they were right or wrong is now something about which we can never be sure.

The Texarkana Moonlight Murders

IRIS HULSE

Texarkana has always been an unusual place. On the east, you have Texarkana, Arkansas, a small town by any other measurement, yet home to the largest population in Miller County. To the west lies Texarkana, Texas, located in rural Bowie County and lucky enough to have its very own Wal-Mart. Together these twin cities make up what is simply referred to as "Texarkana."

Texarkana is a dusty town, built on a foundation of competing railroads and a Mexican border dispute in the 1800s. The town laid low for the next several years, sending off its sons to fight World War I and then II, and welcoming them back home for better or for worse. But no one in Texarkana was prepared for the national attention that came in the spring of 1946. On February 22nd, 1946, a masked serial killer, dubbed the "Phantom Killer" by the *Texarkana Gazette*'s Calvin Sutton, began terrorizing young couples on the town's secluded country roads.

Today, if you search the Internet for information on Texarkana and its morbid history, you will likely be redirected to pages on *The Town That Dreaded Sundown* and its Arkansan producer, Charles B. Pierce. In 1977, decades after the last murders, this film joined the ranks of *Halloween* and *The Texas Chainsaw Massacre* as one of Hollywood's classic horrors, featuring countless local residents as set extras. While the film's accuracy is something to be questioned, it remains a key piece of the town's identity. Visitors can even catch a screening every Halloween at Spring Lake Park, not far from where one of the infamous murders took place.

Texarkana may have embraced its celebrity status, but eighty years ago the town was paralyzed in fear. Within a single spring, five were dead and three were wounded. All in what had previously been a quiet, friendly community.

A Masked Attacker

Just before midnight, on February 22nd, 1946, Jimmy Hollis and Mary Jeanne Larey were finishing up their date in the backseat of

Hollis' father's car. Hollis, 24, and Larey, 19, had been dating for a while, but his parents expected the car (and the lovebirds) home by midnight. Throwing caution to the wind, they parked on a secluded dirt road, known as a lovers' lane, and proceeded to do what young couples will do.

The pair was soon startled by a flashlight, shining through the driver side window and blinding them to whoever stood outside. Hollis quickly composed himself and opened the door, thinking they were being interrupted by an ill-timed police patrol or a prank from some local kids, but they found themselves face-to-face with a masked man holding a gun.

Hollis continued to confront the intruder, telling him, "Fellow, you've got me mixed up with someone else. You got the wrong man." Hollis later said that the masked man muttered something like, "I don't want to kill you, so do what I say." Hollis attempted to calm the assailant, who forced the young man out of the vehicle and demanded Hollis remove his pants, gun pointed squarely at his face. Larey pleaded with Hollis to do as the man said, thinking he would not become violent if they did as he said. Instead the masked man overpowered Hollis, beating him over the head with the revolver. As Hollis lay limp on the cold ground, the attack continued until the sound of Hollis' skull cracking echoed throughout the clearing.

At this point Larey was hysterical with panic, thinking the loud crack of Hollis' broken skull was the sound of him being shot. She told the man they had no money or valuables, attempting to hand the man Hollis' wallet, but he only screamed, "Liar," at her and demanded her purse. Then the masked man told her to run toward the road. Larey ran as fast as she could, but the strange man pursued, continuing to scream, "Liar," at her as she ran.

The assailant eventually outpaced Larey, and forced her to the ground. Larey reported that the man did not rape her, but that assaulted her violent and used his gun to sexually molest her. Larey was afraid for her life, fighting against the weight of her attacker. She eventually managed to escape his grasp, rising up and telling him, "Go ahead and kill me." She then ran to a nearby house at 805 Blanton Street, where she managed to wake up the sleeping woners and pleaded for help. Shortly after, the Bowie County Sheriff, W.H. "Bill" Presley, arrived at what would be the first known Phantom Killer crime scene.

Hollis and Larey were lucky enough to survive this first attack, though they were left with plenty of physical and emotional scars to show for it. Hollis and Larey described their attacker as a tall man wearing a burlap sack with two slits cut for the eyes, though they could not agree on the man's race. Hollis believed the man was white, with tanned skin from working outdoors, while Larey insisted he was a black man because of his mannerisms and "curses." At this point, the attack was treated as a random attempted robbery, it was unknown the chaos that the Phantom Killer would bring in coming months.

The First Kill

In the early hours of March 24th, a truck driver spotted a young man asleep in an Oldsmobile parked on the side of the road. Concerned about the danger of passing traffic, the truck driver ran up to the window, hoping to wake the man and advise him of a better resting area. To the truck driver's horror, the young man was not asleep; he had been shot twice in the back of the head and sat dead in the driver's seat. In the Oldsmobile's backseat was a teenage girl wrapped in a bloody blanket, her body was completely lifeless. These young lovers were not as lucky as the Phantom Killer's first victims.

Richard Griffin, 29, was a retired Navy SeaBee on a double date with his girlfriend of six weeks, Polly Ann Moore, 17, when they pulled over on the highway to have some time alone. They had just finished up dinner with Griffin's sister and her boyfriend at a local café, and Griffin was in no rush to return his girlfriend to her parents' house. Unfortunately, they would never make it home.

Sometime that previous night, Griffin and Moore had pulled over onto the side of the road. It is believed they were approached similarly to the Phantom Killer's first victims, with a blinding flashlight and pointed gun. There was a heavy rainfall over Texarkana that night, so no one would have been out and about to see the killings take place.

Griffin was likely killed first, with two shots from a .32 Colt revolver to the back of his head. Moore, however, had been dragged from the vehicle and sexually assaulted on the cold, wet ground by their attacker. Blood and marks littered the dirt next to the vehicle. After this horror, Moore was also shot and killed by the Phantom Killer. The assailant pulled a blanket from the car's trunk and wrapped her in it before placing her body in the backseat of the Oldsmobile. Any fingerprints and footprints left behind by the killer that night was washed away by the storm.

Griffin's pockets were found empty and turned inside out, and Moore's purse remained at the scene but was emptied of any cash. With the only apparent motive being robbery, questions still remained as to why the crime was carried out so violently. The *Texarkana Gazette*, at the insistence of the Sheriff Bill Presley, made an announcement on March 27th asking residents to not spread rumors or anything else that they did not see with their own two eyes. Despite offering a cash reward, no solid tips ever made it to the police force.

Murder in the Park

Betty Jo Booker, 15, was a straight-A student who was adored by those around her. She worked with Jerry Atkins playing saxophone for a local band, The Rhythmaires, every Saturday night at the local VFW club. On April 14th, she and Atkins, as well as the rest of their band mates, were playing one of their normal shows. Every other weekend, Atkins gave Booker a ride home alternating with a band mate named Ernie Holcomb. This night was Holcomb's night to drive her home, but Booker told Holcomb not to bother because she had a ride set up with an old classmate who was visiting, Paul Martin. Atkins never knew of this change of plans, and until he received a call the next morning he assumed Booker had left with Holcombe, as usual.

Martin's 1946 Ford Coupe was found at 6:30 the next morning by the Weaver family, who were on their way through Texarkana to Prescott, Arkansas. The keys were found still in the car's ignition. Several miles away, in Spring Lake Park, their bodies would be found. Neither the car nor their bodies were anywhere near their destination that night.

Band and classmates claimed that the two were never close to being a couple, and that Booker felt obligated to go out with Martin because of their connection at school. However, no one knows what they were doing pulled over that night, or why they were in that area of town in the first place. No matter what the true story was that night, Booker and Martin would be the Phantom Killer's third and fourth victims.

Like the previous attack, both victims were shot and killed with a .32 Colt semi-automatic revolver. And like the female targets before her, Booker had been sexually assaulted before her murder. After news of the murder was released, hundreds of Texarkana residents flooded the park, hoping to catch a glimpse of the crime scene or help the investigation.

Martin's body was found almost a mile and a half from the abandoned car. He had been shot four times and the ground surrounding his body was covered in his blood.

Booker's body would not be found until five hours later, over three miles from where the car had been found. Booker was found by the Boyd family and Ted Schoeppey, who had joined the community search party to help find the two teenage victims. Booker had been shot twice, and was found with her hand in her coat pocket.

Both bodies showed signs of a struggle against their attacker, yet their fight was unsuccessful. There was no conclusive evidence as to why their bodies were so far from their car.

Booker's missing saxophone played in the running theory of robbery as a primary motive. The police had alerts al over the area, asking people to keep an eye out for a pawned or for sale saxophone matching the serial number of Booker's, and for several months it was considered one of the best leads the authorities had on finding the killer. Unfortunately for the police, on October 24th, six months after Booker's murder, P. V. Ward and J. F. McNief found the saxophone still in its leather case, just yards from where Booker's body had been found. Ward claimed to know what it was as soon as they stumbled upon it. By the time the case and instrument were turned over to the police, the case had already been labeled closed.

A Red Herring

Public panic over the Phantom Killer was at its all-time high when Virgil and Katie Starks were attacked in their modest farmhouse just ten miles out of town. However, questions would eventually emerge over whether this was truly the work of the Phantom Killer, or if someone else was responsible for the crime.

On the quiet night of May 3rd, Virgil, 36, was reading the Texarkana Gazette when two gunshots burst through the front window of their ranch-style home. These bullets hit Virgil in the head, killing him instantly. Katie was lying in bed, already dressed in her nightgown, when she heard the sound of breaking glass. She headed for the living room, where her husband had been seated, only to find him slumped in his armchair, dead. She cried in fear as she reached for the phone, but the attacker shot through her lower jaw, spraying teeth fragments across the Starks kitchen.

In a state of panic and extreme pain, Katie managed to get back up to her feet. She attempted to grab her husband's gun, but was disoriented from being shot. Despite her injuries, she escaped from the house and ran for her sister's down the street. Finding the house empty, she continued to her neighbors' until she found refuge in the Prater house, where the police were finally called. When A. V. Prater answered the door, Katie simply said, "Virgil's dead," before collapsing on the ground. In the time it took for the police to arrive the killer had fled, taking no valuables or anything else of note with him.

Initially, this attack was labeled as another of the Phantom Killer's. It followed the same time pattern as his previous attacks, used a gun as the primary weapon, and targeted a couple. One of the biggest pieces of evidence connecting this attack to the Phantom Killer was a set of unfamiliar tire tracks that matched those found at the other crime scenes. Because of these similarities, many citizens of Texarkana insist that this murder and attempted assault was the Phantom Killer's final blow to the small town's community.

In November 1948, the local authorities made a different conclusion. Another man was arrested and charged with the home invasion and attack on Virgil and Katie Starks. Law enforcement referenced several reasons as to this not being the work of the Phantom Killer, including the fact that the weapon used was a .22 rifle. This change in weapon, as well as the fact this was a home invasion earlier in the evening, pointed police to consider a different suspect entirely.

The town is still home to many skeptics who believe this attack was the Phantom Killer's doing. The crime scene at the Starks home was filled with physical DNA evidence, but at the time DNA testing was only beginning to emerge in the most developed areas of the nation. A little town like Texarkana was nowhere near equipped to handle a case like this, and the DNA evidence was discarded or improperly stored for later testing. While the official stance is that the Phantom Killer was not involved in this attack, the question still haunts many in the area.

A Town In Panic

As the attacks added up, tension in the town of Texarkana grew. After the first and second attack, police forces from both states increased patrols on the town's secluded back roads. A community that had once been friendly, where front doors were never locked and neighbors were always welcome, now grew eerily quiet after sundown.

Businesses saw a decline in customers, especially those catering to the night crowd. Residents were afraid to leave home, even during the daylight, for fear they may become the next target of the Phantom Killer. However, one industry in town became a hotspot for concerned citizens – the local hardware and ammo shops.

Residents bought up guns and ammo like crazy, hoping to be able to defend themselves from the attacks. Deadbolts and other home security devices became commonplace in all the towns households, and some homeowners were even seen setting up booby traps and other contraptions to catch the killer in his tracks.

Many of the town's local high school and college boys rounded up patrol groups. These men would go out at night with baseball bats and other makeshift weapons, hoping to catch the Phantom Killer on the prowl. None of them were ever successful.

Rumors continued to spread and impair the investigations. There was constant news about someone's son being arrested for the murders, or a suspect being charged, but these rumors rarely ever revealed themselves to be true. Police were forced to perform damage control on the stories spreading around town while also conducting their own investigation into the attacks.

Under the Spotlight

After the final attack, at the Starks farmhouse, authorities and media swarmed into Texarkana like never before. The quiet town was buzzing with news reporters from all across the nation, and reports of the murders were spreading to all areas of the country. Texarkana had never experienced the media's curious eye before.

The famous Texas Rangers stepped into the investigation, headed by the well-known Manuel "Lone Wolf" Gonzaullas. Gonzaullas was the first Ranger captain from Spanish descent, and was known for being a ruthless charmer in his day. He spent a great of his time providing interviews for national newspapers and radio broadcasts about the state of the investigation. He was even found one day taking pictures of the Starks crime scene with a young *Life* magazine reporter; neighbors had reported suspicious lights and sounds from the house when Gonzaullas and the woman were found.

While the local press, headed by the Texarkana Gazette, dubbed the suspected serial killer the "Phantom Killer" or "Phantom Slayer," national media clung to a different name: "The Moonlight Murderer." Because of this title, many believe that the murders were all committed under the full moon, when the nights were in fact at their darkest during the time of the crimes.

A Fruitless Investigation

The entire nation was on the lookout for a masked killer terrorizing young couples, with leads coming in from all areas of the South. In all, the authorities considered over four hundred separate suspects, but no one was ever charged with the attacks of that spring. While most of these suspects never received any public attention, the media caught wind of some of the more notable ones.

A middle-aged man from College Station, a Texas town several miles west of Texarkana, was at one point considered a prime suspect. He had previously been caught sneaking up on parked cars, typically with young couples inside, and brandishing a .22 rifle in order to threaten and rob them. While this man was never convicted of murder, many believed him to be the Phantom Killer based on the similar crime and weapon.

In Fayetteville, a young male graduate student of the University of Arkansas committed suicide. In the wake of his untimely death, a note was found containing a handwritten poem and confession to the murders in Texarkana. His military records showed he had showed "homosexual tendencies" during his time with the U.S. Navy, and at the time these tendencies were believed to be a mental disorder related to sexual crimes like rape or assault. Nothing of value ever came from this lead.

Several local residents accused an IRS agent of the crimes, seemingly because of his antisocial demeanor or because he had gotten on the town's bad side. Another man claimed to have committed the crimes during fits of amnesia. Neither of these claims resulted in an arrest.

In 1999 and 2000, several years after the last murder, an anonymous woman called surviving family members of the Phantom Killer's victims, claiming to be his daughter. She apologized for the actions of his crimes and begged for forgiveness from the families. There is speculation over whether these claims are valid, but many believe them to simply be a cry for attention. After all, the primary suspect of the Phantom Killer murders, Youell Swinney, never had a daughter.

Chasing a Criminal

During his time investigating the Moonlight Murders, Max Tackett, an Arkansas law officer, made a puzzling connection. Before each murder a car had been reported stolen and subsequently abandoned on the side of the rode. This information led police to believe that the Phantom Killer was using stolen vehicles to flee the crime scenes, and then dumping them before disappearing into the night.

The next car reported stolen triggered a police stakeout, with law enforcement hoping to find the killer connected to the vehicle. As police closed in on the stolen vehicle, Peggy Swinney was found to be driving. Police seized the car and took Peggy into custody, where she was questioned on how she came to possess the stolen vehicle.

Peggy revealed that Youell Swinney, a known car thief in Texarkana, had given the car to her, but that wasn't all she had to say. Peggy began telling police how Youell was the Phantom Killer, how he had assaulted and murdered all those couples, and how he had made her promise not to tell anyone. She included details of the crimes that had not been given to the public, information only known by police and the killer himself.

Before the police could move in on Youell Swinney, Peggy's story changed. She claimed that her previous confession was a lie, and that Youell was not the Phantom Killer after all. Eventually law enforcement discovered that Peggy and Youell had recently been married, making her unable to testify against her husband at all. While Youell remained an unofficial suspect, it seemed that the police were unable to touch him. But that changed in 1947, when Youell was arrested for auto theft.

At that time, Youell Swinney already had a long criminal record. He had been previously charged with counterfeiting, burglary, and assault, landing him in the Texas State Penitentiary for many years. After his release, he continued his work as a career criminal, but avoided capture for the time being.

During the investigation, police found evidence that Youell had owned a .32 Colt revolver, the murder weapon used to kill the second and third sets of victims, but that he had recently lost the gun in a failed card game. In hi home was also a shirt with the name "Stark" embroidered on the pocket, but it is unknown whether this shirt was actually connected to the Starks murder in the previous year.

With Youell in custody for auto theft, the police attempted to pin him as Texarkana's Phantom Killer. The man had a history of violence and sexual assault, and the record of stolen cars pointed toward his involvement in the murders. Youell never denied his innocence; he simply stayed quiet and refused to work with the police when questioned. A botched injection of "truth serum" during an interview in Little Rock, Arkansas, would eventually end the authorities' questioning of Youell regarding the Moonlight Murders. He was placed in prison for auto theft.

Youell remained in prison until 1973. Many of his cellmates recounted stories that Youell had told them, ones that included intimate details of the Phantom Killer's murder scenes and heavily suggested that Youell knew more than he let on. In 1994, Youell died a free man, never admitting to the Texarkana murders. To this day, most consider Swinney to be the Phantom Killer, even if he never served time for these crimes.

The Missing Woman

On June 1st, 1948, 21-year-old Virginia Carpenter departed Texarkana by train, on her way to her first semester of studying at the Texas State College for Women. She left Union Station at about 3PM, and headed for Denton, Texas and her new life as an educated woman. On the train ride, she met another student by the name of Marjorie Webster, who she shared a taxi with on the way to their dormitories.

Their taxi driver, Edgar Ray "Jack" Zachary, first dropped off Webster at the Fitzgerald dormitories, and then continued on to Brackenridge Hall, where Carpenter would be staying for the term. Zachary reported seeing Carpenter approach two young men in a yellow convertible outside the dorm, saying that she seemed to recognize them and was excited to see them. The next day, Zachary returned to the dorms to deliver some of Carpenter's luggage that she had forgotten at the station. He placed the trunk at the hall's front entrance and left, but no one ever claimed the luggage. That previous night would be the last time Virginia Carpenter was seen.

On June 4th, Carpenter's boyfriend, Kenny Branham, and her mother reported Virginia missing. After being brushed off by authorities, Mrs. Carpenter and other family members left for Denton late in the evening, hoping to help the police find Virginia.

Within several days, there were airplanes, motorboats, and on-foot search parties scanning the surrounding area for any sign of Virginia. Drivers of yellow convertibles were stopped and questioned, and Zachary was questioned by police and subjected to a polygraph test. Carpenter quickly became one of the most famous missing person cases in Texas, with her picture circulating across the country.

Before long, rumors started spreading back in Texarkana. Virginia Carpenter had personally known three of the Phantom Killer's victims, and some started to believe that she had a target on her back. Perhaps the killer had followed her from Texarkana to Denton, just another passenger on the crowded train. Or perhaps the killer was someone that Carpenter knew, like one of the men seen in the yellow convertible to night she went missing. Either way, many believe that this disappearance was connected to the attacks in 1946.

Countless sightings of Carpenter across Texas - riding in a car, buying groceries, or hitchhiking - continued to flow in, but no solid leads were ever discovered. By 1955, Carpenter was considered dead. She had been missing for seven years, and little hope remained of finding her. Despite this, tips continued to emerge on Carpenter's possible whereabouts.

In 1959, a wooden box was found buried with female remains inside that matched Carpenter's physical description. They were sent to Austin for examination, but the landowners soon confessed to digging them up from an old cemetery.

In 1998, a man called the police claiming to know where Carpenter's body was buried. He led police to the grounds of the Texas State College for Women, the school she was meant to attend, but the search came up empty.

Carpenter's disappearance causes some to doubt Youell Swinney's guilt. If her disappearance was a result of the Phantom Killer, the same man who brutally attacked at least three different couples, then this man could not be Swinney. At the time Carpenter went missing, Swinney was being held in prison for auto theft. Maybe Peggy Swinney had a hand in the disappearance of Carpenter, or her abduction was committed by someone other than the Phantom Killer, but it could not have been Swinney.

Phantoms Around the World

Some believe that the Phantom Killer simply moved his crimes to a new location, but it is likely he just inspired other killers to follow his pattern of attack. As the United States reached the height of violent crime and serial killers, attacks cropped up across the country and even abroad. The Phantom Kiiler's *modus operandi* (or M.O.) would become commonplace among serial killers in the coming decades, including the Zodiac Killer, Il Mostro, and the Son of Sam.

In 1946, a young couple was shot in Fort Lauderdale, Florida. Elaine Eldridge and Lawrence Hogan were parked outside Dania Beach when someone approached the vehicle and shot both victims with a .32 semi-automatic handgun. While the weapon used was not a Colt, it remained very similar to the one used in Texarkana. No fingerprints or footprints were found at the scene. With several similarities to the Texarkana attacks, many believed that the killer had relocated across the country. Texas, Arkansas, and Florida police worked together on the investigation, but no major connections were ever revealed to the public.

Located in San Francisco, the Zodiac Killer operated very similarly to the Phantom Killer during the late 1960s. He stalked young people in their vehicles and shot them with a revolver, and his identity remains unknown. However, unlike the Phantom Killer who personally avoided the media's attention, the Zodiac Killer was hungry for exposure. His main source of fame comes from sending cryptic notes to the Bay Area press, including four ciphers. Only one of these ciphers was ever solved, but it led the police no closer to identifying a suspect. These notes were examined top to bottom, in hopes of finding the true identity of the Zodiac Killer, but no leads were ever found.

Across the Atlantic Ocean, from 1968 to 1985, Florence, Italy was shook by sixteen murders. Dubbed Il Mostro or The Monster of Florence, the killer shot young couples parked alone in their cars with a .22 rifle. While four different suspects were arrested and charged with these murders throughout the years, the investigation has attracted scrutiny and many believe these men were actually innocent.

While the Son of Sam's identity is known today, his killings reflected those of the Phantom Killer and others. Operating in New York City in the mid 1970s, David Berkowitz killed six victims with a .44 Bulldog revolver. His attacks triggered the biggest manhunt in New York City, and for years women kept their hair short and avoided disco clubs for fear of being Berkowitz's next target. Like the Zodiac Killer, Berkowitz loved taunting the police and media with cryptic letters, where he promised to continue killing until he was caught. After his capture in 1977, Berkowitz enjoyed a bit of morbid celebrity for his crimes, which many reported he seemed to enjoy greatly. He remains in prison today, serving six life sentences.

While it is unlikely that the Phantom Killer actually relocated to be the Zodiac Killer or Il Mostro, some true crime experts believe it is possible. While the Phantom Killer was one of the first of his kind, looking back his killings were not exceptionally unique by today's standards.

It is easy to see how the Phantom Killer and his Moonlight Murders have shaped our ideas of killers today. Urban legends of a mad man stalking young couples in love, scratching on car doors and leaving bloody hooks behind, persist around campfires and in dark corners of the Internet. *The Town That Dreaded Sundown* might live among the likes of Freddy Krueger and Michael Myers, but it is a fictionalized retelling of the very real horrors that haunted Texarkana that year.

RAILROAD KILLER

They called him the 'Railroad Killer.'

Angel Resendiz earned the nickname because of his penchant for committing his crimes near railroads, using the rail cars as his own personal get-away system.

Committing murder after murder, he was able to elude both American and Mexican authorities for over a decade.

EARLY LIFE

A birth certificate found by the FBI listed his date of birth as August 1st, 1960. He was born To Virginia de Maturino in the town of Izucar de Matomoros in the state of Puebla, Mexico. His mother has stated adamantly that the correct spelling of his surname is Recendis not Resendiz although the killer would have over fifty different aliases throughout his lifetime.

Angel had spent his childhood years with relatives and not with his immediate family. According to his mother, he was sexually abused by an uncle and other pedophiles in the town of Puebla. He would spend his youth roaming the streets, robbing, stealing and sniffing glue. Relatives would later testify that Resendiz was routinely beaten as a child, one time being "jumped" by several other youths who beat him so bad that he bled through his ears. Resendiz would leave home for months at a time then suddenly return mumbling about a coming religious apocalypse.

Legal trouble came early for Resendiz as he was caught trying to sneak into the Texas border at the age of sixteen. This would become the first of numerous run-ins with border patrol agents until he finally made it into the United States, making his way to St. Louis and finding work with a manufacturing company under an assumed name. He even registered to vote with his false identification.

In September of 1979, at the age of nineteen, Resendiz was arrested for assault and car theft in Miami. He was tried and sentenced to twenty-years in prison but was released after only six years and sent back to Mexico.

But he wouldn't stay there for long.

Through numerous attempts of trial and error, Resendiz had learned not only to game the system but to enter and exit the United States with minimal detection.

He learn to use the rail-cars...

AN "INVISIBLE" MAN

Resendiz became so skilled at crossing the border without detection that he began charging for his services. He began to make a living as a human smuggler, transporting Mexicans across the border for a fee.

Resendiz soon developed a reputation for his smuggling skills, often being seen as a 'go to' person in his Ciudad Juarez neighborhood called 'Patria.'

He would make weekly crossings over the border, being arrested only intermittently. He would then be deported back into his native land only to ping-pong back and forth.

Finally, Resendiz would serve prison terms for his crimes. He would be arrested in Texas for false identity and citizenship, getting a year and half worth of jail.

Upon release in 1987, he journeyed to New Orleans and was arrested for carrying a concealed weapon. He received another year and half worth of prison time until parole.

He then went back to his old haunts in St. Louis where he tried to defraud Social Security and receive illegal payments. He got caught and served a three year sentence.

Resendiz then decided small-time burglaries were his deal. He once again illegally crossed the border, journeyed to New Mexico and was caught burglarizing a home. He was imprisoned for eighteen months and upon release he broke into a Santa Fe rail yard, being captured yet again.

"They should have called Resendiz the boomerang man," forensic psychologist Frank Lizzo said. "He knew how to play the game and seemingly had no fear of the system. The system never punished him severely enough for him to stop his crimes, let alone stop crossing the border."

After his last recorded deportation, the killings began.

THE KILLING FIELDS

"He probably started killing somewhere in his late 20s," Douglas said. "He may have killed people like himself initially – males, transients...(he) became angry at the population at large. What America represents here is this wealthy country where he keeps getting kicked out...(he) just can't make ends meet. Coupled with these feelings, these inadequacies, fueled by the fact that he's known to take alcohol, take drugs, lowers his inhibitions now to go out and kill."

Angel's list of victims began in 1986. Continuing to bounce in and out of the United States, he shot a homeless woman and left her for dead in an abandoned farm house. He had met the acquaintance of the woman at a homeless shelter and they became friends. They would later take a trip on a motorcycle together when he felt that the woman disrespected him.

Resendiz would then take out his gun and blow her head off.

The woman allegedly had a boyfriend whom Resendiz shot and killed as well. He said that he dumped his body in a creek between San Antonio and Uvalde. This killing has never been verified aside from what Resendiz revealed to the police during his interrogation sessions.

Five years later, Resendiz would kill Michael White because he was a "homosexual." Resendiz would bludgeon White to death with a brick and leave him in front of an abandoned home.

These were seemingly warm-ups for the more brutal crimes to come which would also include rape.

"Sex seemed almost secondary," FBI profiler John Douglas said when apprised of Resendiz's crimes. "(He is) just a bungling crook ...very disorganized."

Douglas would later concede, however, that it was this disorganization that worked in his favor. Like a true drifter, Resendiz' whereabouts became as elusive as a rational thought in his head.

"When he hitches a ride on the freight train, he doesn't necessarily know where the train is going," Douglas said. "But when he gets off, having background as a burglar, he's able to scope out the area, do a little surveillance, make sure he breaks into the right house where there won't be anyone to give him a run for his money. He can enter a home complete with cutting glass and reaching in and undoing the locks."

"He'll look through the windows and see who's occupying it. The guy's only 5 foot-7, very small. In fact...the early weapons were primarily blunt-force trauma weapons, weapons of opportunity found at the scenes. He has to case them out, make sure he can put himself in a win-win situation."

Resendiz would also leave his weapon of choice up to chance. Whatever the home would have, a statue a mantle piece, a butcher knife, that would become the instrument of murder.

FLORIDA KILLINGS

On March 23rd, 1997, Jesse Howell would be found bludgeoned to death beside the railroad tracks in Ocala, Florida. He was nineteen years old.

"When we got there," Sheriff Patty Lumpkin said. "We see what appears to be a young male, in his late teens or early twenties. Blood around the head area. You could tell by looking at him that he was dead. The first thing I do is make sure that we've got our forensics people on the way, on the medical examiners on the way, and all the investigators that we have called out or either there or en route."

"When those types of things happen it might have been someone who had fallen off a train," Lt. Jeff Owens said. "Or someone who could have been struck by a train."

The authorities quickly ruled out an accident, however, as they examined the body.

"It didn't appear to be an accident," Lumpkin said. "Because if he had been hit by the train the trauma would have been much more extreme. I've seen some deaths from trains and the initial impact from the train would have done more harm to the body."

The forensic team did determine that Howell's body looked as if he were the victim of blunt force trauma.

"We did see a baseball type of cap," forensic scientist Michael Dunn said. "It appeared to have blood on the inside surface of he bill. In addition, there was a pair of wire rimmed eye glasses and one of the eye pieces was missing, one of the lenses was out. This didn't look good either. As we moved closer, we saw that the victim had been dragged to that spot using just the blue jean material around the cuff (of his pants)."

Near the body, they found a brass and rubber coupling. This device was used to link one train car to another. It could also be used as a clubbing weapon.

"It had what appeared to be blood on it (the coupling)," Dunn recalled.

Howell still had jewelry on his person. He wore a gold cross necklace, a watch and a small amount of cash in his pocket. The police ruled out robbery as a motive.

The police did not identify Howell's body right off the bat. They did find a money wire receipt where some money had been wired from Illinois to Florida. The name on the receipt was of a woman named "Wendy."

Police tracked the money transfer to its point of origin which was all the way in Woodstock, Illinois.

Coincidentally, the authorities there were investigating the disappearance of Wendy Von Huben.

Wendy was missing alongside her boyfriend, the nineteen year old Jesse Howell.

"They advised me that they were investigating a John Doe," Woodstock Detective Kurt Rosenquest recalled. "Unidentified male."

Rosenquest then followed up with the investigating team in Florida, sending them the fingerprints and pictures of Jesse Howell.

The Ocala police would then positively identify Howell.

Jesse had met Wendy only months earlier. They had secretly planned to marry and went on a road trip with another couple.

The other couple, however, grew tired of Jesse and Wendy's constant bickering. They demanded to be let out of the car and left. Jesse and Wendy continued into Ocala, Florida where they ran out of money.

Wendy would call her parents in Illinois who would then transfer her $200 via Western Union. The couple would collect the $200 but would not return home.

"We checked Greyhounds," Rosenquest said. "Nobody matching their description ordered buses or train tickets back to the Woodstock area."

Tears were shed as Rosenquest informed Howell's parents that their teen son had been murdered. The investigative team then turned their attention to the disappearance of Wendy.

They held out hope because there were issues between her and Jesse, thinking that perhaps she simply ran off to be by herself.

Police scoured the surrounding areas and used helicopters in all directions around the railroad tracks.

They would find nothing. There was no DNA left behind on Jesse Howell's body either.

Papers and fliers with Wendy Von Huben's information was distributed all throughout Florida up through Illinois.

Authorities also began interviewing the transient population that lived along the railroad tracks.

Two and a half months later, however, Wendy's parents would receive a phone call.

"The phone rang," Rosenquest recalled. "Wendy's father answered the phone. The girl was crying. She said 'I'm sorry. I love you.'"

She would tell the father she was two hours away from Woodstock at a gas station. The father asked for the phone number on the pay phone she was calling from and she said that there wasn't any before hanging up.

The police were not certain that the phone call came from Wendy so they immediately headed out to the gas station where they believe the call took place.

Police tracked down the surveillance video of the gas station. On the video, a woman that physically resembled Wendy entered the gas station.

The phone records, however, revealed that the call did not come from the gas station where the surveillance video revealed a woman who allegedly was Wendy. It came from another gas station where there were fliers posted of Wendy.

Someone had played a cruel hoax as Wendy's parents had added their home number to the fliers

ONE-LEGGED BOB AND A CHANCE DISCOVERY

A year went by without any sign of Wendy.

There was some ray of hope, however, as the railroad authorities called the Ocala police and informed them that the received information from a member of one of the homeless camps. They had a man in custody named "One Legged Bob" who was traveling with a girl and may be responsible for the murder of her previous boyfriend.

"'One Legged Bob' was your typical homeless person," Owens said. "Kinda scruffy. Hadn't shaved in a few days. He had a prosthetic leg that helped him get around. For someone who you might consider crippled, he was far from crippled."

Owens would spend the next eight hours interviewing the only lead he had, a one legged homeless man.

After the grueling interrogation, Owens realized that he had the wrong suspect.

By sheer chance, however, Patty Lumpkin heard about someone they dubbed the "Railroad Killer" during a class she was taking at the FBI.

"They called him the Railway Killer," Lumpkin recalled. "The Angel of Death. He was killing people. Leaving them near the railroad or he was killing them at homes or locations that were close to the railroad.

The FBI knew the Railway Killer as Angel Resendiz.

"We knew that Angel Resendiz was a person that rode the rails across the country," FBI Agent Mark Young said. "We were worried where he'd wind up next. So we decided to make him a top ten fugitive. Maybe the millions of eyes of the public would tell us something."

The strategy worked.

"He was one of the most vile, evil persons that I had ever dealt with," Young said. "It was like every time you turn around there's another murder."

Owens and Lumpkin hoped to talk to Resendiz to query him about Jesse Howell's murder and Wendy Von Huben's disappearance.

"The attorneys representing him at the time in Texas stopped us," Owens said. "They wanted to protect their client from talking. Any defense attorney who represents a criminal will generally tell the person to stop talking to law enforcement."

Resendiz was placed on death row and Texas had a fast execution rate. The two detectives worried that they would lose their chance to interview Resendiz and connect him to the crimes in Ocala.

Owens and Lumpkin decided to mail Resendiz a letter, respectfully asking him if they could interview him. The letter was written in a formal manner and even addressed him as "Senor."

To their surprise, Resendiz responded back and granted them an interview regarding his involvement in Jesse's killing and Wendy's disappearance.

During their meeting, Resendiz was quick to admit that he had killed Jesse. The detectives deliberately withheld information about the killing, holding back details that only the killer would know. But when Resendiz described using a brake coupling from one of the trains, they knew they had their killer.

But they needed to find out what happened to Wendy.

In a follow-up letter, they promised him immunity from prosecution if he agreed to talk. It was a moot point by then as he was already on death row but the detectives still needed permission from Wendy's family to go through with the interview.

In order to receive some sense of closure, the family agreed to the immunity.

"When we get to the prison," Lumpkin said. "We see him coming down the hallway. He (Resendiz) has a waist belt on. It's an electric shock belt and he's chained to the belt. He's just a mild-mannered person but remember that a psychopath or a sociopath doesn't have any feeling. I mean he had dead eyes. He had no feeling in that body. He didn't care about anything."

Resendiz would reveal that he was heading south for work when the train stopped and he spotted Jesse getting off the train for a smoke.

"Resendiz told us that he killed Jesse with a piece of the train coupling," Lumpkin said. "And Wendy was asleep on the train when this took place. And then when they went down the road further somehow he talked Wendy into getting off the train."

Resendiz then raped and strangled Wendy to death.

Resendiz drew a map of where had left Wendy's body. He described burying her in a shallow grave near a canopy of trees. Resendiz would remember that she had a book in a back pack and an army style jacket that he used to cover her fresh grave.

Police would return to the site and were able to locate where he buried Wendy's body. Almost three years after the murder, everything the killer described was still there. The book. The jacket.

And Wendy's body.

"When Wendy ran away she had a small engagement ring," Owen said. "And she had a Winnie the Pooh wristwatch.

The detective would bring those items back to Wendy's parents.

KENTUCKY RAILROAD MURDER

In August of 1997, Resendiz would make his way from Ocala, Florida to Lexington, Kentucky. It was there he would stalk two young college students.

Holly Dunn was a 20-year old junior at the University of Kentucky and it was there she met Christopher Maier.

"Chris Maier was my very good friend," Dunn recalled. "He was just the nicest, kindest man. We decided that we wanted to be more than friends then we started dating. We dated for about three months."

"Chris and I were attending a party. We decided that the party wasn't very fun so we went to go talk a walk by the railroad tracks. We sat down and talked for awhile and when we got up to leave a man came out from behind an electrical box. He had a weapon that he used on Chris. It was some sort of ice pick or screw driver. Something sharp. I guess our immediate thought was he's going to rob us. That's when we realize he wants money we start thinking 'okay, well, you could have our credit card, you can have our ATM card, you can have our car.' Then he started tying up Chris' hands behind his back. And then he came over to me and he took off my belt and that's when I started thinking he doesn't want to rob us."

After tying up Holly, Resendiz then pulled Chris by the shirt across the railroad tracks and into a ditch.

Holly would follow on her knees, pleading for him to stop whatever he was about to do.

"Lie down," Resendiz said, his voice soft but menacing.

"Everything is going to be okay," Christopher said to Holly as Resendiz dragged him into the ditch.

"Shut up!" Resendiz commanded as he gagged Christopher with a sock.

Resendiz then walked off into the darkness. The frightened couple did not know what the psychopath had planned.

"Then he comes with this rock," Holly recalled. "There was no warning, he drops this rock on Chris' head. I'm just thinking 'what just happened?' I don't even know what just happened."

"You don't have to worry about him anymore," Resendiz said to Holly as he got on top of her.

"I went into survival mode, I'm thinking, I mean he's gonna kill me. I may as well fight. I'm gonna fight. He unties my feet and climbs on top of me. I start to kick and scream and hit him but he held that knife or ice pick (to my throat) and said 'look how easily I could kill you.' I stopped everything and then he raped me."

"I memorized his face," Dunn said. "I stared at him and memorized, he had a tattoo on his arm, I was thinking if you have any scars I'm gonna remember your scars, I'm gonna remember your face,I'm not gonna forget it because if I live through this I will get you."

Resendiz completed the sexual assault of Dunn before smashing her head with a rock.

"He hit me five or six times in my face," Dunn recalled. "I think I put my hand up and then I turned over and then he hit me five or six times in the back of my head. He hit me hard. He was trying to kill me. I think I laid there and he thought I was dead."

Resendiz did think she was did as he threw the rock down and ran away from the crime scene.

Holly would suffer severe facial trauma but miraculously survived the attack.

"I had a broken jaw," Dunn said. "Broken eye socket and cuts on the back of my head that they had to staple shut and then I had cuts on my face."

She woke up in a Kentucky hospital, surrounded by family members.

"Everyone was told not to talk about Chris to me. I just said 'Chris is dead, isn't he?' And my Dad actually is the one I said that to and he was like 'yes, he died.'"

TEXAS TERROR

Resendiz would travel to Texas via train and in October of 1988 he flopped down in Hughes Springs. He would enter the home of 87-year old Leafie Mason, attacking the woman with an iron and killing her.

Two months later, Resendiz would sneak into the home of Dr. Claudia Benton, a thirty-nine year old medical researcher who lived in a suburb of Houston near the railroad tracks.

Again, it was a case of a home being to close to the train tracks. The train would provide the perfect cover for the sneaky Resendiz as he realized that the sound of the rail-car racing by would allow him to break in homes without being heard.

He applied the same technique with Benton, breaking into her home, raping then killing her.

Police would find the doctor face down on the floor. Her bedroom soaked in blood, ransacked for any valuables.

He head had been covered in a plastic bag while her body had been covered in a blanket.

"It appears that she (Claudia Benton) was sleeping," recalled Ken Macha, former police sergeant. "He was able to get in and picked up a bronze statuette from the mantle in the living room. He was relentless in beating her. The skull fractures themselves would have been enough to kill her. She was then stabbed in the back with a very large butcher knife."

"Resendiz was brutal, sadistic," said former West University police chief Gary Brye.

Fingerprints and DNA evidence would link Resendiz to the crime.

The problem was they could catch the man that Texas Ranger Drew Carter referred to as "a walking, breathing form of evil."

EVADING POLICE

Seven months later, Resendiz would continue to avoid capture. He remained in Texas, riding the rail cars until coming into the town of Weimar. He would break into the home of Pastor Norman "Skip" Sirnic and his wife Karen. Resendiz smashed a jack hammer into both of their heads, killing them instantly. He would then rape the body of Karen postmortem.

"He would watch these places," prosecuting attorney Devin Anderson said. "He would watch them, wait for them to go to sleep, get in their house and he would strike them before they would even wake up. I thought we have got to catch this guy."

The DNA found at the scene of the Sirnic murders would match those left on Benton. The FBI then realized they had a highly mobile serial killer on the loose...someone who could kill in one town then appear in another town miles away and kill again.

Resendiz was also smart. He would constantly alter his appearance. He'd shave his head. Then his mustache. He'd be clean shaven one week. Unkempt the next. He would wear glasses one week. No glasses the next.

Authorities could not get an accurate description of him other than the fact that he was small.

Resendiz was also able to take advantage of the lack of a coordinated computer system that gave law enforcement the ability to cross-check fugitives. After the Sirnic murders, Border Patrol had encountered Resendiz near the El Paso border but did not find him on the wanted list.

They then deported him back to Mexico.

Within 48 hours, Resendiz was back across the border to resume his killing spree.

"Our computers told us that he was nothing of lookout material," said C.G. Almengor, a supervisor at the border."We really wish he had been in the system so we could have caught him."

Resendiz would be deported no less than seventeen times over the course of his rampage. At no point did authorities make the connection because of his changing appearance, use of different aliases and the lack of a connected system to document illegals trying to come across the border.

A PREFERENCE FOR TEXAS

Noemi Dominguez was a graduate of Rice University who had just recently quit her job as an elementary school teacher to pursue a master's degree.

She was described as "the sweetest, nicest teacher – a darling who went the extra mile."

Fueled by hate, Resendiz would break into Noemi's home and rape her before killing her with a pick ax. He then stole her car and drove to Schulenberg, Texas where he would kill Josephine Konvicka with the same pick ax.

He would leave the weapon embedded in Konvicka's head as well as leave his fingerprints all over the home. He was more than just sloppy, he was getting cocky. He left a newspaper article that described his crimes as well as a toy train...a reference to his nickname as the "Railroad Killer."

Resendiz was also meticulous in approaching his victims.

"He undid the light in her (Noemi's) car," Anderson said. "So when he opened the door it wouldn't come on. That's who were were dealing with. Someone who really knew how to sneak around. Who really knew how to avoid detection."

"He kept killing people. He would not stop. In his mode of transportation, using the railroads was brilliant because they couldn't be monitored. I mean there's thousands of trains and millions of miles of tracks all over the United States."

"I felt hopeless at the time. Because if you're willing to sleep in a train or you're willing to sleep in a field, you can stay lost for a long, long time and I didn't think we were ever going to catch him."

Later that month, Resendiz had journeyed to Illinois, reaching the town of Gorham. He would break into the home of 80-year old George Morber and his daughter Carolyn Frederick. Resendiz would tie Morber to a chair and shoot him in the back of the head with a shotgun. He then raped Carolyn and smashed the shotgun across her head with such force that the weapon broke in half.

Both Morber and Frederick would die from their injuries.

The FBI placed him on their Top Ten list.

They then recruited his common-law wife, Julietta Reyes, and brought her into Houston for questioning from her hometown of Rodeo, Mexico.

Reyes complied with police requests, turning over over ninety-three pieces of jewelry that her husband had mailed to her from the U.S.

Relatives of Noemi Dominguez claimed thirteen pieces. George Benton was able to identify some pieces of jewelry as belonging to his wife as well.

Police would then locate Resendiz's half-sister, Manuela Karkiewicz, who lived in New Mexico. Initially, she refused to cooperate. She worried that the FBI or the police would kill her brother. But Carter convinced her to talk Resendiz into giving himself up.

The FBI knew that Resendiz had made his way back to Mexico after the murders in Illinois and was hiding in his hometown neighborhood of Patria.

Carter was able to get a rapport with Manuela. He convinced her that Resendiz would receive "personal safety while in jail, regular visiting rights for his family and a psychological evaluation."

"I came away with the impression that they (Resendiz' family) definitely had an understanding of right and wrong ... and knew now that what Maturino Resendiz was accused of doing was heinous and wrong ... ," Carter said. "Manuela, especially, came across as a woman of strong faith. There was a very deep emotional strain and burden placed on her in this investigation. She had to make some very difficult choices that impacted her and her family. And, in the end, her actions alone speak to her character."

Carter spent weeks talking to Manuela who in turn "worked a miracle."

They got the serial killer to surrender.

On July 12th, Manuela would receive a fax from the district attorney's office in Harris County which formalized everything that Texas Ranger Carter had promised.

The word passed from Manuela to another relative who acted as a go-between with Resendiz. The relative than came back later that evening and said that Resendiz would surrender in the morning at 9 a.m.

Texas Ranger Drew Carter would accompany Manuela and a spiritual adviser to meet with Resendiz on a bridge that connected El Paso, Texas to Ciudad Juarez.

"When I saw that face there was a little bit of excitement there because I finally said, 'This is going to happen,'" Carter recalled as he remembered Resendiz appearing on the bridge with his dirty jeans, muddy boots and blank facial expression. "He stuck out his hand, I stuck out my hand, and we shook hands."

Resendiz would then surrender to the Texas Ranger.
DEATH PENALTY

Resendiz' attorneys knew that their only hope would be an insanity defense. The Mexican government also got involved, lobbying authorities to spare Resendiz the death penalty

"Insanity was the logical defense because no one wants to believe that there is someone out there who would do things like that," Anderson said. "That was the thing that worried me the most about the case was that jurors would just throw up their hands and say nobody in their right mind could do what he does."

"The thing about what a life sentence with Resendiz would have been, he would have enjoyed it. I mean he would have had pen pals. He would have given interviews if they let him, I mean he would have loved it. And I knew that. And he didn't deserve to live after what he did just didn't. He caused so much pain, so much heartache and so much terror, that's what the whole focus of the trial had to be."

George Benton, the husband of Claudia, would vehemently criticize the Mexican government who support his appeals and domestic opposition to the death penalty.

"(He)looked like a man and walked like a man. But what lived within that skin was not a human being."

"He was small," Anderson said when she first saw Resendiz in the courtroom. "Maybe five- foot five. His forearms though, were roped with muscles. He was scary. Even though he was small you could feel he was dangerous. He looked like a wild animal who'd been caught."

Resendiz looked "timid" in the courtroom and spoke of himself in religious riddles. He claimed he was Jewish and didn't seem effected when he was informed that the prosecution was aiming for the death penalty.

"I don't believe in death," Resendiz, said. "I know the body is going to go to waste. But me, as a person, I'm eternal. I'm going to be alive forever."

The defense said that Resendiz' crimes were caused by head injuries, drug abuse and a family history of mental illness. He has a delusional perception of the world as he believes that he can cause earthquakes, floods, and explosions and that God told him to kill his victims whom they believed to be evil.

He made a living stealing things from his victims and having his wife sell them in Mexico. "That was his job," Anderson said. "And for recreation it was killing the people who lived in the house."

"He was a very intelligent person who worked the system and knew exactly what kinds of things to say to get that defense to work."

The jury, however, would find Resendiz guilty after one hour and forty-five minutes of deliberation.

He was sentenced to die via lethal injection.

"He made it very clear during my conversation with him that he deserves to die," Owens said.

"I want to ask if it is in your heart to forgive me," Resendiz said in his final words. "You don't have to. I know I allowed the devil to rule my life. I just ask you to forgive me and ask the Lord to forgive me for allowing the devil to deceive me. I thank God for having patience with me. I don't deserve to cause you pain. You did not deserve this. I deserve what I am getting."

Resendiz then prayed in Hebrew and Spanish before drawing his final breath.

House of Horror : The True Story of Rosemary West

49

Mary Gilmore

Unfortunately, it's not unusual in this day and time to turn on the news and hear a warning about a new serial killer roaming our streets. It's horrifying and hard to comprehend what could possibly make a person commit such heinous crimes. What is wrong with this person that drives him or her to commit such an act? The truth is that people have searched for the answers to that question for a very long time. Unfortunately, it still remains a mystery for the most part.

Rosemary West is one of those baffling cases. We will look deeper into her life and learn how her inner demons progressed to becoming one of Britain's most notorious and sadistic serial killers, taking the lives of at least 10 young women and girls.

Most of the information obtained by the authorities came from her husband and partner in crime, victims who escaped or were permitted to leave, and a great deal from her own children. Rosemary has offered very limited insight into the story, even to this day.

Remarkably, she did not act alone in committing these grisly deeds. This story is immensely complex, which I will attempt to sort out and then tie it all together with the union of Rose Letts West and Fred West in their vicious killing spree. There will be accounts of child abuse, rape, sexual deviance, torture, and murder. Rosemary West's crimes were so horrendous; it may be difficult for some of you to read.

Rosemary West's Early Life

Rosemary's mother came into her room one morning to wake her for school. Rosemary probably knew by the familiar expression on her mother's face that this would be one of those mornings that fills her life with constant dread. As she gets dressed, she begins preparing herself for what she knows is probably about to occur.

As she walks into the kitchen, breakfast is the last thing on her mind. Instead, she braces herself for the punishment she is about to receive. Don't misunderstand, Rosemary hadn't done anything wrong, but her father didn't need a reason.

His kind of punishment wasn't a time-out or a swat on the behind as most children receive. His were the kind that affect a child for a lifetime. Rose has no idea whether she is about to be beaten or if she'll endure other horrors that her father is known to inflict.

That is a likely scenario in the life of Rosemary West. Her father was a paranoid schizophrenic. The mental illness along with other problems, made life for her, her mother, and her siblings a nightmare. The abuse was bad enough, but what made it even more terrifying was not knowing from one minute to the next when or why her father's rage would erupt.

As a result of her home life, Rose made bad grades and became overweight. To make her situation worse, she was teased and bullied at school, giving her no relief from the continuous damage to her self-esteem.

There's a possibility that Rosemary's destiny was sealed much earlier in her life. It's not surprising that Rosemary's mother suffered from severe depression. The illness was so debilitating that she received electroconvulsive therapy several times while Rosemary was still in the womb, one of which occurred just before Rosemary's birth. There were some that thought this therapy was the reason for Rosemary's frequent outbursts of anger as well as her inability to do well in school.

Most of us would be unable to imagine a childhood such as the one led by Rosemary West.

Why do They Kill?

There are no exact traits of a serial killer to help us understand what drives them to kill. Some of them come from a two parent loving home while others have divorced parents. Some had abusive parents and others had loving parents.

Some think it's due to a head or brain injury sometime in their life; however, most people that have had brain injuries do not become killers. The majority of serial killers are men who act alone. Rosemary is not only a woman, she also had a partner in her life of crimes. Female killers and couples represent only a small percentage of serial killings.

The Federal Bureau of Investigation did a symposium, which was comprised of 135 experts who have dealt with serial killers in various ways to determine commonalities of serial killings. They determined that there are no definitive common traits. However, the central nervous system is constantly developing in adolescence, which determines a person's social coping system. That is, they develop the way they interact with their peers such as in negotiation and compromise. If it does not develop adequately, it can result in violent behavior.

It would be safe to say that the events of Rosemary West's childhood could be a factor in the choices she made later in life.

Rosemary's Life Before the Murders

Rosemary Letts was the fifth child born to Bill and Daisy Letts in Devon, England on the 29th of November in 1953. She normally went by the shorter version of her name, Rose. As we've seen, Rose's childhood was unlike most other children's. In pictures of Rose at a younger age she had an ever present smile on her face. You wouldn't guess that she was going through hell within the walls of her home.

The Letts family lived in Northam, a charming seaside town in Devon. Neighbors thought of Bill Letts as a nice man; however, they must have thought it strange that they rarely saw his children. When they did, the children were mainly seen walking around in their garden. One neighbor stated that they really didn't seem to be playing at all. They were just walking around and rarely seen outside the walls of the garden.

What they didn't know was that the children weren't allowed outside the walls and were afraid to play because they were forbidden to get dirty.

Although Rose's father constantly punished the children including Rose, he was not as physically abusive with Rose as with his wife and the other children. It was thought that he didn't physically abuse her as much as the others because he thought there was something not quite right about her.

Some people thought that he didn't hurt Rose as much because he was using her for his sexual pleasures instead. Others speculated that Rose learned at a very young age that she could control her father's anger by using sex.

Rose's mother Daisy, eventually left her father. She moved out of their house taking Rose and the other children with her, freeing them from the abusive environment. Remarkably, after a brief time, Rose moved back in with her father who resumed sexually abusing her.

One day, as Rose waited for a bus, she was approached by a man. Rose described him as a dirty man who had disgusting green teeth. She and the man struck up a conversation and even though his appearance was repulsive by most people's standards, Rose became attracted to him. The man's name was Fred West.

West was raising his daughter and stepdaughter at that time so Rose began babysitting the two girls. In addition, Rose and Fred also became a couple.

Fred's Early Years

Fred West, the son of Walter and Daisy West, was born in Much Marcle, England in 1941. He was the second of their six children. Growing up, he was considered to be a nice boy. They appeared to be a normal family, however, Fred's upbringing was perhaps even worse than Rosemary's. According to Fred, the motto around his house by his father was, "Do whatever you want, just don't get caught."

Fred would later reveal to police that incest was a common occurrence in his household. He said his father regularly had sex with his own daughters. Fred also claimed that his father introduced him to bestiality. In addition, it was thought that his mother Daisy took his virginity when he was 12-years-old.

Not surprising, Fred did not do well in school and dropped out at the age of 15. Two years later, he was involved in a tragic motorcycle accident. He received a broken arm and leg and a fractured skull. The head injury put him in a coma for eight days. Afterward, his family claimed that thereafter, he frequently become enraged without warning. Amazingly, two years later, he received another head injury. In this instance, he fell from a fire escape causing unconsciousness for 24 hours.

Fred's history of child abuse and head injuries would certainly coincide with the conceivable characteristics of a serial killer.

At the age of 20, he was caught and arrested for molesting a 13-year-old girl who subsequently became pregnant. He was convicted, but for unknown reasons he was not sentenced to prison. The reason is possibly because the girl's parents and Fred's parents were friends. Even with his family's propensity for deviant sexual acts, they had recently decided to try their hand at getting religion, therefore, they disowned Fred after this latest incident.

Fred had problems keeping a normal job. He landed a construction job; however, he was caught stealing. In addition, he continued to get caught molesting more young girls. It's amazing how he could still be roaming the streets even back at that point.

Shortly after, when West was around 21, he ran into a former girlfriend named Catherine Costello. She was better known as Rena, which was the name she used while prostituting and the name stuck. In addition, Rena was an accomplished thief. Nevertheless, even with her reputation, she was described by neighbors and other acquaintances as a very nice person and an exceptionally good mother.

Even though she was already pregnant with another man's child at the time, things heated up between her and Fred again and they married about two months later. The baby girl was born in February

1963 and was named Charmaine. Rena had another child by Fred a year later and named her Anna Marie. You will hear the names of these two girls in a shocking context later in the story.

Unbelievably, someone gave Fred West a job driving an ice cream van. This wouldn't seem a proper job for Fred the child molester to say the least. For Fred, it was the perfect job with young girls running after him. It was an ideal way for him to find victims.

While working at this job, a four-year-old boy ran into the street in front of his van and the child was killed. After this incident, even though the death was accidental, Fred feared people in the area would seek retribution for the boy's death. He thought it would be in his best interest to move away.

At the time, a woman named Isa McNeil was caring for the West's children. Additionally, Rena had become friends with a young woman named Anne McFall. They all moved with Fred to *The Lakeside* caravan park in Bishop's Cleeve, Gloucestershire, which is where Fred would later live with Rose.

With Fred's sadistic habits still intact, there were soon problems in this odd household. Fred insistently pushed his warped sexual necessities onto all three women. It became too much for his wife, Rena, and the children's nanny, McNeil, so the two of them moved to Scotland. On the other hand, the other woman, Ann McFall, had warmed up to Fred and stayed behind. Besides, she had already become impregnated by him.

Fearful of Fred, Rena and Isa's planned was to keep their departure secret from him and sneak away. Unfortunately, McFall told Fred, which enraged him. He allowed them to leave, but not with the two children, so the two women fled to Scotland. Rena returned frequently to visit her children.

After that, McFall began to pressure Fred to divorce Rena and marry her. Apparently, this didn't set well with Fred. When she was eight months pregnant with Fred's child, she completely vanished. She was never reported missing, but her body was later discovered in a field minus her fingers and toes, which had been removed and were missing.

Fred was left to care for his daughter and stepdaughter.

The Evil Duo Unites

Around this time is when Fred met Rose at the bus stop. It was at the time when Fred was caring for his step-daughter and biological daughter, so Fred already had at least the one murder of Anne McFall under his belt when he met Rose. Rose then began taking care of the two children.

When they first got together Rose was only 16-years-old and Fred was 12 years older at 28. Her father absolutely disapproved of the relationship. He threatened West that if he didn't leave Rose alone he would call Social Services due to Rose's young age. That was ironic since her father had been having sex with her himself for a long time. Of course, that was most likely the reason he didn't want her to go.

Nevertheless, Rose moved in with Fred and they lived together as a family with Fred's two daughters. After only about two months, they married she moved in with him at *The Lakeside Caravan Park* in Bishop's Cleeve, Gloucestershire, where Fred had lived with Rena and Anne.

Of course Fred, a man of few scruples, soon introduced his young and damaged wife to a sadistic world of pornography and urged her into prostitution. Due to Rose's demoralizing childhood, it didn't take a lot of urging for her to become caught up in his world.

Not one to hold down a regular job, Fred's contribution to the income was mainly by thievery. He wasn't very accomplished at that either and was frequently caught and arrested. It wasn't long before he was sent to prison for 10 months, leaving young Rose in charge of his two daughters.

To make matters worse, she had become pregnant and gave birth to her daughter, Heather, in 1970 while Fred was still in jail. Being young in addition to having mental problems, caring for three children was a tall order for Rose and she didn't handle the situation well, to say the least.

To add to the pressure, seven-year-old Charmaine, began to be unruly and Rose was unable to cope with it. Years later, according to the other child, Anna Marie, it was not unusual for both girls to receive severe beatings; however, no matter how bad the beating, Charmaine refused to cry. This infuriated Rose so it's no surprise that Charmaine didn't seem to be around any longer after that.

This is thought to be when Rose committed her first murder. Rose's tendency to lose her temper most likely caused her to loss control and kill Charmaine. Apparently, Rose hid the girl's body, because it's known that Fred disposed of the body after he returned from prison.

Fred would hold this over Rose in the future. On one of the occasions when Rose's father tried to convince her to leave Fred and come home, Fred made a remark that was something like, "Come on now Rose, you know what we have between us." For someone that didn't know Fred, it would sound like an expression of love. More than likely with Fred, it was his not so subtle way of saying, "You can't leave. I have too much on you." She later told her parents that Fred would do anything, including murder.

Fred's first undertaking after returning from jail was to dismembered and dispose of Charmaine's body. For whatever sick reason, as with Anne McFall, he removed her fingers and toes and then buried her. This became the normal process in Fred's body disposal. It was later speculated that Fred and Rose were possibly involved in Satan worship. It is thought by some that removing the fingers and toes of their sacrifices was typical for Satan worshipers.

The next time Rena Costello came to visit her daughter it naturally created a problem when she discovered her daughter's absence, thanks to Rose. As you can imagine, Rena was not happy about her missing daughter and demanded some answers. Therefore, Rose and Fred must have decided that Rena would have to go as well. So this visit to see her little girl resulted in Rena's demise as well. Minus her fingers and toes, she was buried in a field close to the Caravan Hotel where Rose and Fred still lived.

That meant a total of at least three people had already lost their lives courtesy of Fred and Rose West. One each for Rose and Fred and now Rena by both of them.

A brief time later, Rose gave birth to their second child, Mae. They bought a large two-story house in Gloucester; however, there was not much money coming in. Fred started putting up panels in the rooms to create multiple bedrooms called bedsits. They were tiny rooms, which didn't fit much more than a bed. They began renting out these rooms for extra income; however, the rooms served another purpose as well.

By this time, Rose's fulltime career had become *prostitute*. They also began working other women out of the house. One of the rooms labeled "Rose's Room" was dedicated to Rose for turning tricks. Outside the door was a red light, which was lit when the room was in business. The children knew they were not to disturb when the red light was on. The room also came complete with a peephole, which was Fred's method for watching his wife in action and for making videos.

Both Rose and Fred had come from a family where incest was normal. It was not unnatural to them when Rose's own father occasionally came to their house to have sex with her.

In around October of 1972, Rose and Fred hired Carol Owens as a new nanny for their children. She told her story years later stating that Fred and Rose attempted to bring her into their twisted lifestyle. Not wanting any part of it, she soon left their house.

A few weeks later, as she was walking home, Fred pulled up beside her and offered a ride. The next thing she knew he hit her on the head. When she awoke, her hands were tied and Fred was in the process of taping her mouth.

She was told that if she tried to resist, Fred would call in his friends and let them have their way with her and she would then be killed.

They said they would bury her under the paving stones outside their home along with hundreds of other girls. Terrified, she didn't attempt to resist.

Unbelievably, they allowed her to leave the next day and she proceeded to file charges on them. Fred somehow managed to convince the court that the sex was consensual. In addition, Owens decided that testifying against these two could be an unhealthy choice.

The couple was given a meager fine on a charge of indecent assault and then released. She would be the last victim that the Wests' would allow to leave alive.

Years later, she regretted not testifying. She felt that if she had, it could have saved the lives of numerous women and girls and she was most likely correct.

One day, Fred and Rose arrived home and their neighbor, Elizabeth Agius, was outside. She had become friendly with the couple, so Fred stopped for a chat. Just in conversation, she asked what they had been doing, so Fred proceeded to tell her exactly what they had been up to.

He said they were cruising around looking for young girls. He must have felt he needed to explain why his wife would go along with him on such an outing. He said they figured the girls would see Rose and wouldn't be scared to get in the car. She would later say that she thought he must be joking...he wasn't.

Meanwhile, Fred was busy redecorating the cellar. One of the prostitutes that worked in the house later told authorities that she saw black suits, masks, chains, and whips down there. Fred had created his own torture chamber.

Anna Marie, Fred's remaining child with Rena Costello, was the first to be brutalized in Fred's torture chamber. She was bound, gagged, and violently raped as Rose watched. She was only eight-years-old at the time and this treatment would continue for years.

Eventually, Anna Marie moved out of the house to live with her boyfriend, which quite possibly saved her life. Again, letting her go would prove to be a bad move for the Wests later in court. As one of the survivors, a considerable amount of the horror stories came from her.

After Anna Marie's departure, Fred's attentions naturally turned to his daughters Heather and Mae; however, Heather wanted no part of it and resisted. Understandably, she was unable to keep it to herself and told a friend about the horrors happening at home. This would seal her fate, but Fred later claimed to police that her death was accidental.

The life of Rose and Fred West continued filled with the unimaginable. They would go on to have a total of seven children who were born in a short time span. It is believed that three are by Fred, one is by her own father, and the remaining three are from her clients. It almost seemed that their reason for having children was so Fred and Rose would have someone to torture at the times when no one else was tied up in the cellar. You can certainly say with certainty that Fred and Rose West were definitely not loving parents.

The One's That Didn't Survive the Terror

Over the next few years, the abuse of the West's children continued as did the murders of others. At some point, Fred went to work at a slaughter house. It was thought that this is when his already violent habits became even more gruesome. It could have been a factor in his fascination for dismembering his victims.

It is believed the next victim was Lynda Gough who was a personal acquaintance of the West's. She enjoyed participating in some of their sexual activities by sharing sex partners with Rose. However, for unknown reasons she later vanished. Gough's mother came to the West's house looking her daughter and was told that she moved in order to pursue a job. While she was speaking to the woman, Rose was wearing some of Linda Gough's clothing.

Carol Ann Cooper, only 15-years-old, is thought to be the next victim. She disappeared while walking home from the movies.

Evidence showed she died by strangulation, was dismembered, and buried in the garden.

Lucy Partington was in town visiting her family and a friend over the Christmas holidays. She went to the bus station to take a bus back home and most likely Fred, being one to hang out at bus stations asked her if she wanted a ride. As Fred and Rose planned, it is thought that the only reason she let them even approached her was due to the presence of Rose.

It is thought that they kept Partington in captivity for about a week after she vanished because poor Fred showed up at the hospital about a week later with a large laceration needing stitches. Authorities think he received the cut while cutting up Partington.

Shirley Hubbard went missing when she was returning home from Droitwich. There was definitive evidence of her torture. Her head was completely wrapped with tape with only a short rubber tube in her mouth to breath.

Juanita Marian Mott was a former tenant of the Wests'. Her torture was obvious. She was gagged with a binding made of socks, tights, and a bra, which were all stuffed inside each other. She was also tied up with clothes line rope looped around her thighs, arms, wrists, and ankles. This was done with the rope going back and forth around her horizontally and vertically until she was completely immobilized. She also had a rope with a noose, which most likely suspended her from the rafters in the cellar.

Shirley Anne Robinson was one of the prostitutes that worked out of their house who had sexual relations with both Fred and Rose. She became pregnant by Fred, at the same time Rose was pregnant by one of her clients.

Shirley began to get the idea she would like to replace Rose, which is not advisable in this family. Rose demanded that she had to go. She and her unborn child were dismembered and buried in the back garden. The cellar was full of bodies by this time and the back garden became the new burial grounds.

Therese Siegenthaler was a hitchhiker in route from London to Ireland. Some of the evidence showed that like Partington, she was kept alive for close to a week during which time she was likely tortured and raped.

Allison Chambers was the last known non-related victim. She was killed in 1979.

Their oldest daughter, Heather Ann West, was the last known victim. Fred claims he killed her by accident. His story of the "accident" went something like this. He told police that Heather was being extremely insolent so he had to slap her. She then started laughing at him so he was forced to grab her by the throat to stop her from laughing. He said that unfortunately, he must have grabbed her too tightly because she began to turn blue and stopped breathing. He tried to revive her by putting her in the tub and running cold water on her, but it didn't work.

He then removed her clothes and attempted to put her in a garbage bin, but she didn't fit. Back into the tub she went so he could make her smaller, but he first strangled her with a cord to make sure she was dead. He told police he didn't want to start cutting her up and then have her come alive on him.

He also closed her eyes before he started cutting. He said he couldn't dismember her while she was looking at him. He must have been hearing a strange sound because he told police he found the source of a noise when he cut off her head. He said it was a horrible and unpleasant sound like scrunching. He also said that after cutting her up, she fit quite nicely into the garbage bin.

She was later put in a hole that the West's son, Stephen, had dug with the intention of it becoming a fishpond. Fred put Heather in the hole and built a patio over it. Stephen had unknowingly dug the grave for his own sister's burial.

Police also believed that they killed 15-year-old Mary Bastholm in 1968, though they never found her body. The Wests' son Stephen, later told authorities that he believes Bastholm was one of his father's earlier murders because his father boasted about it.

The Evidence Begins to Surface

Oddly, they violently murdered many of their victims, but then set others free after they had finished using and abusing them. Naturally, some of them went to the police.

The released victims were some extremely lucky women to say the least. Their reports finally got the attention of a Detective Constable named Hazel Savage. Savage was also familiar with Fred West and his arrests for thievery and child molestation through the years since the time he was married to Rena Costello.

Fred videoed an incident in which he raped Anna Marie while Rose held her arms. Anna Marie told friends about her home life who in turn told their parents. This and other information got back to Savage.

This enabled the Detective to obtain a warrant to search the West's property. It was the beginning of the needed evidence to finally remove these damaged and dangerous monsters from the unsuspecting public.

Fred was arrested and charged with rape and sodomy of a minor and Rose for assisting in the rape of a minor. Amazingly, Fred and Rose West were still not suspected of murder. At this time, the younger children were removed from the home.

Due to the evidence found in the home, Detective Savage had the suspicion that there was more going on here and she began digging deeper into this strange family. She had a feeling that there was something suspicious concerning the whereabouts of their daughter Heather and she was determined to find out.

For instance, it was noticed in the videos of the West's and their children that was seized from their home that Heather was never present. Also, in interviews with some of the children, they said something that should not come from the mouths of children.

Apparently, there was a common joke around the West house. Fred told the children that he would buried them under the patio with their sister Heather if they didn't behave.

Unbelievably, the case fell apart when two of the main witnesses decided not to testify. Detective Savage continued questioning the children repeatedly to no avail. Fred and Rose had programmed them and put enough fear in them by then that they would no longer say anything to help the case.

However, the evidence together with case workers reporting the family joke about their sister Heather kept Detective Savage searching. It also appeared that another child, Charmaine, was missing as well. Eventually, Savage put together enough evidence to obtain a warrant to dig on the Wests' property.

Soon after that, Rose answered the door to find the police with warrant in hand. She quickly called Fred to tell him the police were about to dig on their property and they're looking for Heather. It turned out that Fred would be of little help because it took him four hours to get home. He came up with some excuse about passing out due to inhaling paint fumes at work.

Could it have been that Fred was busy disposing of evidence such as fingers and toes or perhaps he had a burial he had not gotten around to completing. That will never be determined.

They began searching the house in addition to excavating the garden in February 24, 1994. The dig was originally intended to search for the body of the daughter Heather, which they soon found. Fred was brought in by the police for questioning the next day. He surprised the police by confessing to the murder of his daughter Heather and he repeatedly told police that Rose knew nothing about it.

Fred and Rose must have been up all that night getting their stories straight. It is thought that Fred assured Rose he would take all the blame and she shouldn't worry. Fred was good to his word, at least in the beginning.

Meanwhile, after the attending pathologist began inspecting the bones of Heather, he brought it to the attention of the police that there was an extra leg bone indicating the presence of at least one other body.

After that discovery, Fred decided he should do some damage control by telling police the location of Alison Chambers and Shirley Robinson's bodies. He hoped this would prevent them from doing any more digging.

It was first thought that Fred did this to avoid being categorized a serial killer, which is someone that kills more than three people. Unbelievably, as it turned out, Fred wanted the police to stop digging because he didn't want his cherished home to be torn apart any further.

Nevertheless, they continued and began to find more human bones. Rose was not arrested until around March 4, 1994. Even then, it was only for sex offenses. Fred had trouble deciding for sure if he wanted to protect Rose after all. He would go on the recant his confession that he killed Heather and then later changed his mind again saying Rose was innocent.

In Britain, prisoners are sometimes assigned an "appropriate adult", which is someone that assists and basically befriends the prisoner. This was normally done for juveniles; however, Janet Leach was assigned to Fred. Leach didn't know she was about to become the confidant of a serial killer.

It turned out that Fred became comfortable enough with Leach that he soon told her the whole gory story. She pointblank asked him if there were more victims. Fred responded that there were six more and went on to draw a sketch of his house and garden complete with the locations of the graves.

Fred knew exactly where they were located; however, he had some trouble remembering all their names. He recalled one that had a scar on her hand; therefore, Scar Hand became her name. Another he called Tulip because he thought she was Dutch, although she was actually Swiss.

Fred was now on a roll and confessed to the murders of his ex-wife Rena Costello and ex-lover, Anne McFall. He told leach that he dumped them nearby his childhood home. He then confessed that he buried his step-daughter Charmaine, Fred's child that Rose killed, close to the hotel where they lived in Gloucester. Strangely, Fred would admit to the murders, but he would not admit to the rapes.

Meanwhile, Rose continued to play the role of an innocent woman, denying any involvement in the murders. She went so far as to act horrified at the actions of her perverted husband. When Fred attempted to contact her, she snubbed him not wanting to have anything to do with such a despicable person.

After making bail, Rose moved into a halfway house with her son Stephen and her daughter Mae. The police were not convinced of her innocence and bugged the house. Nevertheless, Rose stuck to it and never spoke of anything that would involve her in murder. Only charges of sexual offense remained against her.

As can be imagined, the town of Gloucester was flooded with the media. The attention had a tremendous impact on the small town. The West's house became known by the appropriate name "The House of Horrors". The residents were in disbelief that this unimaginable crime spree had gone on in their town for 20 years.

The Trial

As it turned out, Fred took the easy way out. He hanged himself in his jail cell by tying together bed sheets leaving Rose to deal with the whole state of affairs.

She was finally charged with 10 of the murders since Rena Costello and Anne McFall were before she was on the scene. She went to trial in October of 1995.

One after another, witnesses took the stand and told their shocking stories. One of the highest drama moments of the trial came with the testimony of Fred's oldest daughter, Anna Marie. She was on the stand for two days. At one point she looked her stepmother straight in the eye as she told a story of sexual abuse and torture that began when she was a little girl of only eight-years-old.

She recalled the incident when she was so savagely raped by her father while Rose held her arms. During the incident, Rose was telling her how lucky she was to have parents to show her how to please her husband when she gets married. She said she was hurt so badly that she couldn't attend school for several days. She also recalled a day that her father strapped her down and raped her while he was home for a quick lunch break. These were only two of the many horror stories she lived.

The second day of her testimony was delayed for several hours because she took an overdose of pills the previous evening.

Another person that offered a wealth of damaging testimony was Fred's *Appropriate Adult* and confidant, Janet Leach. However, she became so stressed that she suffered a stroke during the trial causing another delay. It wasn't until later after the trial's end that Leach could tell police the entire story that Fred confided in her.

One of the key witnesses was Carol Owens who was one of the girls they brought home under the pretense of being a nanny. She was allowed to leave, but only after she endured their sadistic sexual torture. Needless to say, she had tales to tell.

Another witness who is still referred to as Miss A was lured to the West house and saw two naked girls who were being held prisoner. She watched as they were tortured and raped. She was then raped by Fred and sexually assaulted by Rose. She was one of the lucky ones that left that cellar with her life.

It wasn't hard for the jury to come back with a unanimous verdict of guilty on 10 counts of murder. Rose received life in prison.

The Aftermath

The "House of Horrors" at 25 Cromwell Street in Gloucester where nine bodies were found was demolished in October of 1996; however, there seemed to be a curse that affected many of the people associated with Rose and Fred West.

John West, Fred's brother, hanged himself while awaiting his trial for the rape of his own niece Anna Marie.

Anna Marie continued to suffer from the memories of her distorted childhood. In 1999, she attempted suicide by jumping from a bridge. She was rescued, leaving her to live another day with the memory of the horrors from her past.

Stephen West, the son of Rose and Fred, attempted to commit suicide in 2002 in the same manner as his father and uncle by hanging himself. However, it wasn't meant to be because the rope broke.

The actual number of murders will remain a mystery. During his interrogation by the police, Fred stated that there were two more bodies buried in shallow graves that they would never find.

He also told them there were 20 other bodies spread around in various places. He claimed he would show the police the location of one body each year. One wonders if he knew at that time that he would later take his own life and wouldn't be following through with that promise.

Fred took any other secrets he had in his evil little mind with him to his grave. After that, Rose wasn't interested in discussing the matter any further.

According to an article in the DailyMail, dated February 2014, even though Rose West filed for a couple of appeals after she went to prison, she has now decided she never wants to leave her top security jail cell at Low Newton jail in Durham and why would she, her cell is equipped with TV, radio, CD player, and private bathroom. She has never confessed to committing any murders.

Authorities know the women and girls were tortured, raped, killed, dismembered, and buried; however, they don't know the details of many of those crimes. Rose has been asked by numerous people to give those details, but she refuses.

Conclusion

This is an account of actual facts; however, it hard to believe that it's anything other than a fictional horror story.

Even after hearing about the disturbing childhoods of both Rose and Fred West, it's difficult to understand the extent of their warped minds. Even more disturbing is the fact that two people that are this broken can find one another and carry out their evil deeds together.

This story brings us no closer to the answer of what drives serial killers. Both Rose and Fred were abused as children mainly by their fathers; however, it was young women and girls that were the focus of their punishment.

There have been books and a movie made about them to show us how this horrific story unfolds. However, only in our minds can we come close to conjuring up the evil that occurred within the walls of 25 Cromwell Street. We may never know the full extent of the terrors that transpired.

The fact that Fred West is gone and Rose West will never see the light of day should make us all sleep a little more soundly.

A MOTHER'S KILLER : THE TRUE STORY OF JENNIFER BAILEY

70

AMBER ULLMER

Imagine coming home after a hard day of work through the door to your quarter of a million dollar home. Then, hearing an eerie silence and nothing but darkness surrounding every inch of your four bedroom, two bathroom, roomy home. With a passing glance to the dining room and living room of your 3400-square-foot house, you head up the stairs with the goal of taking a warm bath and getting a fresh set of clothes for the night.

This is what Susan Bailey[1] did just before it happened. Two dozen stab wounds and two slashes to her throat cut that goal short with a spattering of blood on the wall and a coagulating pool of blood beneath her. She didn't expect to be killed that night. Neither did she expect it to be her own children who would do it to her.

Susan Marie Bailey grew up as a bubbly, funny, outgoing, and smart kid, according to her mother, Kate Morten. She had curly dark hair, was the second of four kids, and was extremely musically talented with the violin and clarinet. Susan was always a people-person. She wanted to do something at the intersection of business, fashion, and people. So, she went to college and earned a business and accounting degree at her local Minnesota college.

To get her fashion experience, Susan worked at Levi Strauss & Co. while in college. She still wanted to get out there more. Her life was a struggle in Minnesota with the snow stomping on her every attempt to be successful. She couldn't make it to work during the winter and work didn't stop just for the weather.

Susan had a difficult time commuting to work. She had to struggle through twenty miles of snow and ice every day. Months and months of brutal winter weather created snow drifts and blinding blizzards that became a routine. She requested to be moved to a closer store which they allowed her to do. Even though it became easier because she didn't have to drive that far in that bad of weather through the winter, it

---

1.   http://www.apple.com/

wasn't any easier in the Spring. An extra 28 inches of snow replaced pleasant Spring weather.

Then, one time when she had to close up shop after the other customers left and the cleaning had been done, she locked the front door and discovered an empty parking lot. Well, almost empty. Snow took over everything in sight, including her car.

Snow chilled her to the bone, darkness swallowed the town, and she was all alone. The snow was so high that she couldn't even open the doors to her car to get inside. So, she called her parents from a pay phone in a state of panic. She cried and in a fit of shivering from the cold she told her mother, "I'm never going to spend another winter in Minnesota." She did just that.

With that, Susan moved to California and built a successful clothing store. Then, she met her husband, Richard Bailey. Not so long after, she called up her mom with a startling message. "Mom, I'm married," Susan told her mother over a phone call in 1988, "Richard and I eloped."

Richard worked in the military and Susan was forced to follow him around while he was in the military. After he finished with the military, he took over caring for his kids and Susan worked. She worked extremely hard and took good care of her kids: Jennifer and David.

She worked two jobs to make sure that her kids could have anything and everything they ever wanted. Problems started when Jennifer was 18 and she wanted a 16-year-old guy named Paul Henson Jr. He was into Satanism, songs about death, and role-playing games. Of course, Jennifer's mother wasn't so thrilled about this and forbid her daughter to see the boy.

Similarly, 14-year-old Merrilee White wanted to be with Jennifer's boyfriend and she was willing to go to great lengths to do so. Her mother, Amy White, also didn't like Paul and told her not to see him. Meanwhile, little David Bailey just wanted to make his sister happy who oftentimes had to take care of him because the mom worked so much.

According to Donna Fielder, author of "Ladykiller," Paul Henson convinced the two that he had two personalities. Apparently, each girl was dating one of them.

Jennifer was scheduled to begin at an art college in a few days and the other three were supposed to start at Northwest Independent School District. Under the veil of appearing to be innocent teenagers, the four of them plotted for days. They planned on killing their parents so they could all be together, drive to Canada, and live happily ever after.

Paul, a 16-year-old with a double personality in which one was an executioner from the 18th century, had been dying to kill someone anyway. He wanted to know what it was like. So, Merrilee attempted to stab her sleeping mother who luckily talked her out of trying to stab her, Paul waited at home with a gun for his parents, and Jennifer Bailey waited at home for her hard-working mom to get home so she could kill her.

Jennifer Bailey was the only successful one out of the three. Susan Bailey was just coming home after leaving her second job in Fort Worth, Texas for the day. She returned home just in time. Jen, Paul, and David took turns stabbing Susan 26 times[2] in the throat after Paul's attempt to kill his parents didn't work.

On September 29, 2008, 11:31 AM, it was reported that 43-year-old Susan Bailey was found dead in her Roanoke home. The Tarrant County Medical Examiner's office claimed that she had multiple stab wounds to her neck. According to star-telegram.com[3], "Sgt. Chris Almonrode said officers had visited her home in the 200 block of Oxford Drive on Friday at the request of the woman's mother, who had grown concerned after not hearing from her daughter. He said

---

2.   http://donnakayefielder.blogspot.com/

3.   http://star-telegram.com/

officers could not get an answer at the door and found no evidence indicating that anything was wrong."

Kate Morten, Susan's mother, tried calling her daughter from her home in Minnesota. When no one answered, she called the Roanoke, Texas police. No one came to the door of their upscale home, so the Roanoke police burst into the door and found a murder scene.

They found the mother's body upstairs in the hallway sitting in a pool of her own blood. Foul play was immediately suspected as the cause of death. The Texas officers also found a bowl of poisoned pudding, a chunk of hair, and an electrical cord dangling right into a bathtub. Inside the bathtub sat three phones and a knife under a foot of water. Jennifer and David were going to kill their mother one way or another.

Meanwhile, a curious South Dakota cop [4]stopped Susan's car for violating town curfew and couldn't believe what he found. He pulled over Jennifer Bailey, 14-year-old David, and 16-year-old Paul in Susan's 2002 Saturn. He pulled them over at a closed gas station where they were trying to steal gas. They didn't have any money and their stories didn't make much sense. They had no real plan either.

He took them to the station and called the police in Roanoke, Texas. They knew about the kids and the woman that the car was registered to. The Tuesday before that week, Paul's father reported him a runaway and thought he was at Jennifer's house. The officers did not find him there. They did find his packed bags and a driver's license. Later on that day, they came back when Susan found a loaded magazine for a pistol, but the police couldn't find the gun.

Roanoke officers quickly put the pieces together after hearing that the three were together in Susan's car. At first, they didn't go straight in when the mother called worried about Susan because no one came to the door and the car was gone. When they found out about the kids,

---

4.   http://www.apple.com/

that's when they went in through the house through a window and found the dead mother.

The officer called Roanoke police and upon hearing what was happening, he held the three on suspicion of capital murder. They were all held at a juvenile detention facility in Sioux Falls, S.D.

Paul wasn't able to kill his parents, they decided to stay out late for a dinner and a movie, thankfully. Merrilee White, on the other hand, didn't get to kill her mother Amy White because luckily, she woke up before she could. The 15-year-old Fort Worth girl was detained on the 23rd of September after her mother reported that she woke up and found the girl standing over her with a knife. Merrilee was demanding that Amy give her her car keys. The girl later admitted to the police that she wanted to take her mother's car so that could take her friends to Canada.

When authorities went to investigate[5], they found notebooks, binders, and handwritten papers, computers, and discs that police described as, "pertaining to the preparation of murder." In the boyfriend's home, they found handwritten notes, papers, computers, discs, and "The Demonic Bible." As mentioned earlier, Paul loved to practice Satanism and was fond of all the things any parents wouldn't want their 17-year-old to be into. He was an avid fan of role-playing and fantasized frequently. Only, this wasn't done as a result of the fantasizing mind of a deranged 17-year-old; it was real.

On September 23rd, police called the Bailey home because they were looking for the boyfriend who was reported as a runaway. Susan and Jennifer fought over Paul. Police later came back later when Susan reported finding ammunition. The police searched the home and found a butcher knife in between the couch cushions and a knife under Jennifer's bed. Jennifer was showing signs of plans to kill early enough

---

5.   http://www.nbcdfw.com/news/local/

Affidavits_4_Teens_Planned_To_Kill_N_Texas_Mom.html

that it could have been prevented. However, her sweet mother had no clue that Jen would actually kill her.

Their school district, Northwest Independent School District, commented on this in an article published on September 29th in 2008 at approximately 11:31 AM. They said, "Our thoughts are with the families involved, and our school personnel continue to focus on the education and well being of our students. Should any child or staff member need to talk about the situation, school counselors are available." Too bad their counselors didn't notice earlier how unstable these four children were. Susan Bailey might still be alive.

Donna Fielder, as mentioned later, spoke to Kate, Susan's mom, who said that she still couldn't believe that her grandchildren would do such a terrible thing. Kate lived through the moment with baited breath from the phone call that drew silence from her deceased daughter to the announcement that her grandchildren killed their mother, her daughter.

What happened to the other three kids? [6]Jen stayed in the Denton County jail without bail and the boys stayed at the Denton Country Juvenile Facility. All three faced capital murder charges. They even tried to try Paul as an adult. In this case, he would serve out his Juvenile sentence and then finish up his sentence as an adult afterward. Under normal conditions[7], juvenile offenders were released from Texas Youth Commission when they would become adults so they could serve out the rest of their sentence. Davide was tried under state's determinate sentencing statute.

Paul got 60 years in prison[8], Jennifer got 60 years in prison, and David only did his juvenile term then went on to live as normal a life

---

6.	http://www.nbcdfw.com/news/local/

Affidavits_4_Teens_Planned_To_Kill_N_Texas_Mom.html

7.	http://crimeblog.dallasnews.com/2008/12/roanoke-woman-indicted-in-moth.html

8.	http://www.apple.com/

as he could have. When police asked Jennifer about her motive, she simply said, "We did not see eye to eye."

It seems like such a small charge for murderers. Would a life-sentence have been more deserved? Probably. Did they get a light charge because they were only kids? Most likely.

My Life of Crime [9]laid out the details in regards to the three murderers. Jennifer Bailey is a white female born on October 5th, 1990. Her maximum sentence date is September, 26th, 2068 which she has been sentenced to spend at Hilltop Unit. Hilltop Unit[10]. is a correctional institutions division (prison) located at 1500 State School Road, Gatesville, TX 76598-2996. It can be found three miles outside of Gatesville.

On The Texas Tribune[11], Jennifer Bailey is listed as being located at the Mountain View Unit for committing "LESSER INCLU MURDER committed on 9/26/2008 in Denton County" for which she is serving a "60-year term" beginning on "9/26/1008."

She is listed as a female, at 25 years of age, found in Mountain View under 01621147, from Denton county, and born 10/5/1990. She is white, 5 ft 5 in, 122 lbs, with blonde hair and hazel eyes.

Her parole eligibility date is 9/26/2038.

On *Denton County, TX Jail Records*, Paul Allen Henson Jr. is listed with the aliases of "Talos, Malaki, and Scai" with an SO# of 164000, and he is described as a white male with brown hair/eyes standing 6'3" at 145 pounds. He was booked at the Denton County Sheriff's Office on 06/09/2009 for capital murder by terror threat/other felony. His offense date is 09/26/2008. Because he has to spend 60 years in jail, he's looking to be released 9/26/2068.

---

9. https://mylifeofcrime.wordpress.com/2012/12/07/kids-that-kill-jennifer-bailey-david-bailey-and-paul-allen-henson-jr/

10. https://www.tdcj.state.tx.us/unit_directory/ht.html

11. https://www.texastribune.org/library/data/texas-prisons/inmates/jennifer-bailey/727001/

A few years later, Candice Delong sat down in an interview with Jennifer Bailey for the details on Jennifer's perspective that night when they killed Susan Bailey.

During the video,[12] Jennifer says that she went upstairs and started feeling doubtful. She went upstairs to the bathroom and looked at herself good in the face. Jennifer knew she would have to look at that face for the rest of her life and the decision she was about to make.

She questioned if she really wanted to kill her mother. She explained, "That is when I made the decision that I was going to tell my mom what was going to happen and then call the police regardless of the consequences." She then said that she was too late. She heard a scream that broke her thought processes. She went out to the hallway and found her mother pushed up against the wall by Paul who had one hand around her throat and a knife in the other.

Jennifer Bailey then says that her mother told her to "call the police." She adds, "Then I said no."

Explaining why, she said, "Because, at the same time, Paul pointed at me and said, 'Don't!' And to this day, I have no idea why I said, 'no.' After I said, 'no,' Paul just grins and pulls the knife across her throat." From there, Jennifer and David helped finish the mother off. With that, they took off with the mother's car, no money, and whatever gas was in the tank to get them to Canada.

Donna Fielder, the woman who originally covered this story when working at the local newspaper in the Bailey's hometown, recalls the event in September 2008 that ended with the death of Susan Bailey at the hands of four teenagers. She explains how the four of them: Jennifer Bailey, David Bailey, Paul Henson, and Merrilee White tried to kill their parents and steal whatever money they could from them before taking their cars they planned on driving all the way to Canada from Texas.

---

12.   http://www.investigationdiscovery.com/tv-shows/facing-evil/videos/jennifer-bailey/

She recalls that the four teenagers plotted against Susan Bailey, a hard-working mother, and the long journey they made from her death to that run-down gas station they were pulled over at.

Jennifer Bailey, David Bailey, Merrilee White, and Paul Allen Henson enacted one of the most violent crimes in US history to a woman who did not deserve such an attack. It was such a popular case that filmmakers have taken to the story and made video-enactments of it such as *Deadly Women,* a series that took Jennifer Bailey's story and portrayed her as a young girl who fell in love with a pagan, Paul. Paul convinces Bailey to kill her mother and run off with him. They plan on running off to Canada together, but it doesn't quite go as planned. The mother tells her they cannot speak and havoc wreaks as Paul tells Jennifer that she needs to brutally murder her mother.

Susan Bailey was a hard working mother of Jennifer and David who had anything and everything they ever wanted until Paul came into the picture and what they had was just not enough.

Jennifer and Merrilee were bound so tight under the spell of Paul and David just wanted to make his sister happy. With that, they took a sharp blade and took away Susan's life and breath. They tried to get away and enjoy a happy life in the cold of Canada, but they lacked a plan and cash to make that fantasy a truth.

Perhaps this was all the will of a psychopathic teenager who thought he was two people. Sadly, he ruined the lives of two young girls and a young boy to fulfill his disgusting fantasies.

To this day, David and Merrilee sit alone and forgotten and without the ones they loved. Jennifer and Paul await 52 years more of time to stare at bars and cement walls. David lost a sister, a mother, and two friends. Merrilee lost three friends and the trust of her mother. Paul lost two loving parents and both his girlfriends. Jennifer lost the most: her boyfriend who she cared for dearly, her mother, and her self-worth.

The moral of the story? The all-American family, neighbors, children aren't all that movies and books make them be. Darkness taints the pages of every good storybook.

A MOTHER'S KILLER :

THE TRUE STORY OF NICOLE KASINSKAS

82

CHRISTINE GOODMAN

Nicole Kasinskas was a quiet, unassuming teenage girl. She was born and raised in Nashua, New Hampshire to Anthony Kasinskas and Jeanne Domenico.

"I lived with both of my parents and my younger brother until I was eleven years old," Nicole said. "And my parents divorced and my Dad moved out."

"I think after my parents got divorced and I was dealing with that, I became a little bit angrier. I had a little bit more resentment towards him, and it did change my perspectives about myself and about life in general, I guess even as an eleven year old."

In May of 2002, she found "romance" as a fifteen year old on-line with eighteen-year old Billy Sullivan.

Sullivan lived in a town called Willmantic where he worked as a line cook at McDonald's.

"Nicole hadn't had a lot of boyfriends," prosecuting attorney Kirsten Wilson said . "She was really caught up by the attention by this guy who was saying amazing things to her about how beautiful she was and what she meant to him."

They would communicate daily through e-mail, letters and phone calls. Despite not having met in person, they both declared love for each other within days, speaking of marriage and planning their future together.

"They filled in sort of the gaps of everyday communication and relationships with fantasies and making these assumptions on who the other person was," Wilson said.

"He lived in Connecticut and so our relationship was almost one hundred percent over the phone," Nicole said. "But it became everything to me very quickly because of the amount of attention that he paid me, and I didn't really feel that I was getting that from anywhere else."

Nicole had been vulnerable to Sullivan's Internet advances as she was a loner with very few friends in high school. She was routinely bullied at school by other girls. On one occasion, she was walking down the hall and one of her bullies had pulled her sweatpants down to her ankles. Nicole was not wearing any underwear, furthering the humiliation. Nicole refused to go back to school the next day after that incident.

"The bullying at school certainly made Nicole vulnerable to someone like Sullivan," forensic psychologist Fiona Russo said. "She's lonely, she's being picked on at school and completely humiliated. She stuck to herself and so when some guy pays attention to her, even when it is only online, her fantasy life goes into overdrive. She's able to project things on him that he doesn't deserve or merit."

The more severe the bullying became, the more Nicole began to withdraw and cling to Sullivan.

"As I got older, it was easier for me to isolate from people," Nicole said. "I think at that point I had just gotten used to being more alone as opposed to being around people. And it just became a part of who I was. Maybe if I was more open or maybe if someone had tried harder to reach out, that it could've been different."

Nicole's mom, Jeanne, was her best friend. Jeanne worked at an elementary school for a period of time, holding down such jobs as a crossing guard, a lunchroom monitor, and a paraprofessional for about three years before taking a job where she worked on group contracts for the Benefits, Brokers and Administration department.

"Jeanne Domenico was well loved in the community," Wilson said. "Hard worker. Really sort of a bright, energetic, sweet woman. She was trying to make her daughter happy."

Despite the bullying at school, Nicole got straight A's at school and made her mother happy whenever she made the honor roll.

"School really became my self-worth and I really identified with, like whatever my grades were," Nicole said. "However I was doing in school I felt it reflected on me personally, because I felt that it was so much a part of who I was. I never got in trouble in middle school. I never got spoken to. I never had a detention. It never really crossed my mind to do anything that would be against the rules."

"It would have been helpful if there was more of an acknowledgment that I was doing so well. I think it also would've been helpful if there was more involvement with guidance or something. Just more of a like a check-in...see how things are going."

"Somehow, someway, Nicole got lost in the cracks," Russo said. "That in no way justifies what she did. It may be how she justified it during this time. Her parents are divorced. She doesn't see her Dad. Her mom is working all the time. There had to have been days where she felt intense loneliness Going to school just to be ignored or bullied. To a fourteen year old girl you really may not see the light at the end of the tunnel. So you seek an outlet. Some turn to drugs. Nicole found her own drug in the form of the words that came out of Sullivan's keyboard."

MOTHER AND DAUGHTER TROUBLES

At least on the surface, there were no problems between mother and daughter.

Until Nicole ventured on-line and met Billy Sullivan.

Her mother found out about the relationship and wanting to make her daughter happy, drove the young teenager out to Connecticut so she could meet Sullivan for the first time.

"This was a two hour drive from Nashua to the place in Connecticut where Sullivan lived," Russo said. "It is easy to say here is where Jeanne made a fatal mistake. But in her mind, it is all innocent. Her daughter is fourteen and begging her to drive out to meet this guy. Begging and begging. Until she finally she relents."

More visits followed but friends and classmates knew little of the teen's relationship. Sullivan had informed some of his friends that he had a girlfriend that was "out of state." Other than that, he revealed very little about his personal life.

"He's quiet, he didn't really like to talk," recalled Danny Goss who was a classmate of Sullivan. "But he was good in school and didn't get in any trouble."

"I think the relationship intensified to a degree that Jeanne herself didn't anticipate," Russo said. "And it is easy to play Monday morning quarterback here but there had to have been some kind of father figure present to say 'hey, this is an eighteen-year old working at McDonald's. You are a fourteen year old honor student. You have a future. Don't blow it on this guy. But it isn't like teens listen to you anyway."

The two teenagers soon discussed the prospect of moving in together. Her mother quickly objected to this idea as well as nixing the idea of Nicole sharing a joint bank account with Sullivan.

But the young man later stayed overnight one weekend with Nicole's mother's full consent.

The relationship is the first for Nicole. She pedestalizes Sullivan as everything she has fantasized about is coming true.

"Nicole had a void in her life," Russo said. "When her parents divorced it certainly affected her psychologically in the way she viewed men. Then along comes Sullivan whose older and more experienced. She gets the love from him that perhaps she sought from her father. The older man, wiser than his years, showering her with attention. She was vulnerable to that."

"Her father didn't have too much to do with her after the divorce. She had that longing in her heart for that male figure. And along came Sullivan."

PERSONAL DEMONS OF HIS OWN

Sullivan, however, had his own personal demons he was fighting.

"He did have mental health issues," Wilson said. "He had been hospitalized a number of times. During high school he had some behavioral issues. Some anxiety, that kind of thing."

It was later revealed that Sullivan had been on numerous psychiatric medications to curb his depression, anger and schizophrenia. He had been weaning himself off the meds, however, and on one occasion he engaged in an argument with Nicole's mother over dinner.

Jeanne had asked Billy if she liked the dinner she had prepared. He said yes and then Jean made the comment that "I bet you don't get that too much at home."

Sullivan was highly defensive over anything that involved his home life. When Jeanne made that comment, he turned hostile.

"Sullivan was protective of his home life," Russo said. "If anyone insulted his mother or if he even perceives that someone is insulting his mother then he gets abusive. He did this to Jeanne, who had obviously made nothing more than an idle comment. That was the first warning sign and the relationship should have ended then and there."

Nicole, however, defended her young beau and from that moment the tug of war for her heart began.

"Nicole's own naivete comes to bore at this point," Russo said. "She has no experience with boys and here is this older guy that she looks up to, almost as a father figure of sorts, who turns her against her own family. Against the one person who loved her the most. Her mother. It is a tug of war that the mother loses simply because her daughter's hormones are raging and she doesn't yet have the emotional capacity to know any better."

After a year of dating, in August of 2003, Sullivan drove out to Nashua to spend a week with Nicole. By this time, they are both fed up with Nicole's mother's objections to their ideas of cohabitation.

"Our relationship was definitely emotionally abusive," Nicole said. "And I think now over time, from looking at it, my perspectives on that have changed so much. I feel like he is responsible for his actions and I am responsible for mine. I didn't really get that and I feel like in order to be emotionally abused, in order to stand for it and stay in it, there's gotta be something missing in you. There's gotta be something hurting already, something is not there, something's not right. And that needs to be figured out, found and fixed. Regardless of how a child is acting or what's coming off,there's more inside that kids need help with or guidance or just to have some type of connection with someone. You need to have relationships with people ahead of time, so that when the bad stuff does happen does happen you don't just come in to it expecting to work it out. Like, you need to have firm foundation with that person in order to work it out."

Nicole continued to side with Sullivan against her mother. The two argued constantly, Sullivan's influence quickly become apparent in Nicole's attitude toward her mother as she found fault with everything she did.

The two teens began discussing an unheard of option.

They began discussing the prospect of killing her mother.

"Well, this is where it starts getting...it's a scary business for me," Nicole said in a jailhouse interview. "I'll tell you that. I feel like I"m gonna cry. I don't talk about this stuff so this is really the first time. I think that my relationship with my mom was good. It was fine. I loved my mom. And...that changed. When...I'm not saying I stopped loving my mom, but...our relationship changed. I'm not gonna say that we were the most open because we weren't. We didn't talk about every little thing. I don't remember ever once talking about my parents' divorce with either of them. But the thing is, we didn't really talk about much of anything. When I was fourteen, I became involved with seventeen year old boy. This is really stemming into why I'm here (in jail) now."

OUT OF CONTROL

"Emotions begin to run high as Sullivan ups the ante in his hatred for Nicole's mother," Russo said. "Nicole is emotionally underdeveloped and has to choose between her mother and her 'man.' It is easy to look at it hindsight but with the teenaged girl's warp logic, she sees Sullivan as her entire world now. So she will do anything for him. Even murder."

Nicole's mom really didn't realize the danger that Sullivan was. She began doing what every mom does, demanding that her daughter stop seeing him, stop chatting with him and concentrate on her schoolwork. Nicole, on the other hand, remained fervent in her desire to move to Connecticut to move in with Sullivan.

"Jeanie, rightfully so, said 'you're fifteen you're finishing school,'" Wilson said. "'You're not moving to Connecticut' and that really upset both Nicole and Billy."

The prospect of not seeing Nicole had an adverse emotional effect on Billy.

"He started talking about killing himself...on the road...driving into a big truck because of leaving me..because of his sadness over it," Nicole recalled. "And I think now it just sounds silly, you know? But it wasn't then, and it was terrifying to me because I didn't...I didn't know how to...because of the way that our relationship was. Because he had become so much a part of my life. I mean, I really didn't feel like I was anything without him. I had nothing in my life at that time...I felt...at that time. So the thought of losing him in that way just wasn't okay with me. And that is unfortunately when conversations started about ultimately what happened. I guess I really I don't really go into too many details but I was sixteen and he was eighteen at that time. And I guess I should give you some background. He killed my mom and I was a part of it. I was not physically there but I knew and I helped him. I was, you know, going through the motions of what was being done. But mentally and emotionally, I don't think I was fully there. I don't think I was fully getting it."

"It was emotional manipulation," Russo said. "It is all so scary romantic for a fifteen year old girl to have some guy who is so in love with her that he is going to kill himself because he can't be with her. She has no one in her life to say 'this guy is a loser nutcase.' There isn't anyone that can talk sense to her. So she falls for the emotional manipulation of a highly disturbed but cunning con man."

Billy had convinced the depressed Nicole that her mother was an obstacle to both hers and his happiness.

"I really just did whatever I could to maintain that relationship because I didn't want to lose that," Nicole said. "I didn't want to lose him. And I quickly learned how it would go if I didn't always do everything that he wanted me to do. At that point...you know, getting to be fifteen...sixteen years old...I would fight more with my mom and there was a lot more to fight about, especially with, you know, this relationship that I was having with this kid."

THE FINAL PLAN

The couple tried different methods to murder Jeanne Domenico.

First they tried to poison Jeanne's coffee. The teens had placed Dimetapp, Benadryl and other drugs into Jeanne's coffee creamer in the refrigerator.

Jeanne used the creamer but didn't die and evidently remained ignorant of the plot on her life. The teens then added bleach to the creamer, wanting to strengthen the amount of poison. It was unclear in a court affidavit if Jeanne ever drank from the spiked creamer again.

The next idea was to set Nicole's mattress on fire with a candle. That idea didn't work because the bedding was made of fire retardant material.

It is unclear how the teens planned to fire up the mattress, whether they sneaked into her Nicole's bedroom and tried to fire up the mattress while she slept.

The third idea was to blow up the fuel oil tank in Jeanne's house. The teens had tied two ropes together which would serve as a wick. Their idea was to set fire to the rope which would then ignite a fire from the fuel tank. This idea was of course unsuccessful.

"These were hair-brained schemes from the start," Russo said, "particularly the fuel tank episode. What is interesting is that these are passive attacks. There is no face to face encounter with the mother, they just really want her gone. But it does show how these were test-runs of sorts. Sullivan was working up his nerve to do something violent. Nicole was building up her psyche. With each unsuccessful dry run, their determination and focus to do the job became greater until finally they realized that physical violence would be the only alternative."

THE ATTACK

The couple decided that Sullivan would do the killing. Nicole waited in the car at a local 7-Eleven where he mother worked part time to make ends meet. She wanted to wait there because she hated her home so much. Her boyfriend obliged, and entered the home of Jeanne Domenico between the hours of six and seven in the evening, waiting for her to come home from work.

The plan was for Billy to kill Jeanne by hitting her on the back of her head with a baseball bat.

Nicole waited anxiously in the car for an extended period of time then began to get worried as to why Sullivan was taking so long.

"Nicole called him and asked him what was taking so long," Wilson said. "Jeanne began getting upset that Nicole wasn't home and kept saying 'where is she? Tell her to come home.'"

Nicole heard her mother's voice on the other end of her cell phone telling her to "come home."

As became her habit, she did not listen to her mother.

"Sullivan did not attack Jeanne immediately," Russo said. "Again, he needed that fuel to add to his fire. So he confronted Jeanne, asking her why they kept refusing them to be together. Jeanne would speak logically like any adult would. She's underage. She's still in school. Of course, none of this would get into the head of Sullivan."

Jeanne made the mistake of turning her back on the young man. He then hit her across the back with the baseball bat.

"It looks as if Jeanne tried to get out of the kitchen door," Wilson said. "Billy started grabbing kitchen knives and attacking Jeanne with the steak knives from the state clock in the kitchen."

The attack was, in a word, brutal.

Sullivan stabbed Jeanne numerous times near her heart and stomach. He stabbed with such ferocity that the blade broke off the knife and he had to retrieve another. Then he stabbed her eight times in the throat.

"A number of the steak knives snapped off during the course of the attack," Wilson said.

According to later testimony by Sullivan, Jeanne managed to get a hold of one of the knives and tried to fight back. At this point, however, she is stunned and bleeding. Sullivan realizes that he is in trouble and goes in to finish the job.

Sullivan stabs her repeatedly as Jeanne tries to get away. A blade enters her lung.

"I'm done," were Jeanne's final words.

He then changed his clothes and cleaned the blood off. He then went back to Nicole, telling her to go inside the house to check for any weapons that he may have left behind. He also told her to get a towel.

The murder complete, Sullivan returned to the vehicle and announced that he had done the deal.

The couple, however, had a deal. It was now time for Nicole to do her part. She would help clean up the evidence left behind.

"The fact that she could go and clean up after Billy had killed her mother," Wilson said. "She had to have hit her mother with the door. And then she had to have stepped over her body to clean up for her boyfriend. That she was able to do that was chilling to do me."

Nicole took a cloth and began clean up her mother's blood from the kitchen floor.

"The fact that a psychopath like Sullivan was able to stab Jeanne to death isn't the most blood curdling aspect of this case," Russo said. "The really scary part is how Nicole was able to go back into that house, see her mother laying in a pool of blood on the kitchen floor, then begin to do her end of the bargain, which was to clean up after her boyfriend. The amount of psychological and emotional disconnect here is chilling."

The two then hid the evidence in the outskirts around town before going to a shopping mall in order for Sullivan to purchase new clothes.

Hours after the killing, Nicole finally began to realize the gravity of what has taken place. She realizes that she and Billy were not going off to "see the world." Her best friend, her mother was gone forever.

Jeanne's body would be discovered by her boyfriend later that evening and he quickly called the police. At around 10:15 p.m., Sergeant William Moore and Detective Shawn Hill saw Sullivan and Nicole approach the crime scene.

"They were cocky enough to think they could outwit the cops," Russo said. "By approaching the crime scene and acting all innocent, not knowing what happened, they thought they would deflect attention away from themselves. It really shows you how dumb these two kids were."

The police then stated the teens would have to be separated for an interview. Nicole protested, stating that Sullivan would not know how to get to the police station. The police informed her that they would take him there themselves.

"This is when things start to go haywire in their heads," Russo said. "Nicole is getting nervous, knowing that they will be questioned separately and face the prospect of not having their stories straight. These two were not exactly forward thinking individuals."

The two waited for the police cruisers to arrive and made conversation with Detective Moore. The detective noted that Sullivan did most all of the talking and admitted that he did not like police officers, stating that he had been charged before with crimes he did not commit.

Moore informed Sullivan that he would be given a "fair shake" in the questioning.

Sullivan, however, kept talking. He informed the detective that he had been shopping for souvenirs with Nicole that day and talked about Jeanne's relationship with Nicole. The detective said that Sullivan paced back and forth and then sat down on the trunk of his car.

Twelve minutes later, Detective Linehan arrived on the scene, making contact with both Nicole and Sullivan. Linehan noticed how nervous and "jumpy" Sullivan was. Linehan told Sullivan to "relax" and then the teen explained that he suffered from anxiety but did not need medication. He told the police that he had "no problem" to come to the station for questioning.

Linehan sat with Sullivan in the back seat of the squad car as they headed back to the station. Both of the teens were having casual conversations with the officers but after being questioned separately, they both admitted their involvement, leading police to the locations where they had disposed of the evidence.

"Both of the teenage lovers wilted under the police interrogations," Russo said. "She immediately ratted out Sullivan as the killer while he did the same to her. There was no loyalty for one another while under the police questioning."

Sullivan would be convicted of first degree murder, sentenced to life without parole.

Sullivan, however, did not let his Lothario ways go to rust in jail. He wrote love letters to a girl named Monique Teal who was then sixteen. This occurred while Sullivan was awaiting trial and later Teal's testimony was used in court.

Teal, using a pen name of Monique Sullivan in her love letters to Sullivan, had agreed to a date to marry the now twenty-year old murderer. Teal's mother, however, found out about the letters and forbade him to call or write.

"He just laughed about it," she said. "He said that no matter what my mom would say or do that nothing could keep us away from each other."

"You see him trying the same techniques on Teal," Russo said. "The immediate declarations of love. The flowery language. The idea of them against the world. In Teal's case, however, her mother put a stop to it."

Sullivan admitted to the Jeanne Domenico killing in one of his letters to her, Teal would reveal, although she didn't read from the letter in court. She said she obeyed Sullivan's demands and threw that letter away.

JAIL LIFE

Nicole Kasinskas would plead guilty to second-degree murder.

"My original sentence was forty years to life," Nicole said. "It is now thirty-seven years and a half to life based on a plea that if I acquired my GED I would get two and a half years off. I don't mark days off on my calendar. I don't do those types of things. This is my life now and I want to live it. I don't want to just look at it as one day down closer to my real life. Like this is my real life. I smile a lot and I live a lot and I'm happy a lot and I just prefer it that way rather than get lost in the sadness of it because you can. And I have. But if I...if I can choose not to...if I can be stronger than than then I want to. And it makes me feel freer. It makes me feel that I have more control of my life."

"Her life as a promising honor roll student at fifteen years old with her mother who loved her very much," Wilson said. "She lost her entire life. And for what?"

"I had no goals. I had no hopes and dreams, you know? You need to have your own hobbies and friends and stuff. Outside the relationship, there needs to be that balance. I just never had that, I never figured that out."

"Maybe if someone had said something like, 'I see you, I see that there's more to you than this and I want to see more of you. I'm here for you. I care about you.' I mean everyone needs help, everyone needs support."

BLACK WIDOW : THE TRUE STORY OF MARGARET RUDIN

97

BRIANNA VALDES

Margaret Rudin, dubbed the Black Widow of Las Vegas, went on trial on February 26, 2001 for the murder of her fifth husband, real estate king Ronald Rudin. After a lengthy, chaotic trial and her defense claiming that involvement in illegal activities resulted in Ron's death, the jury found her guilty on May 2, 2001. In August, the court sentenced Margaret Rudin to life in prison with the possibility of parole in 20 years.

According to reports, Ron Rudin went missing about a week before Christmas in '94. He paid a visit to wife Margaret Rudin's antique shop, in the same plaza as his real estate business. Officials said that Margaret Rudin did not report Ron missing until a few days after he disappeared. She told police she thought nothing of it at first because, aside from Ron being upset with her after an argument, he seemed like his usual self.

About a month after Ron disappeared, a couple of civilians stumbled upon human remain near Lake Mohave in Nevada. Police found ashes and fragments of bones in the burn pile. However, the skull, which was inches away, remained mostly intact. It had at least four bullet holes, which forensics later matched to a .22 caliber weapon. Police made two trips to the house, and on the second visit, they found blood on the walls, photographs and items removed from the house including a mattress and carpet. However, though the police suspected that Margaret Rudin killed her husband, the evidence up to that point was circumstantial at best.

A year and a half year later, a diver found a .22 caliber gun with a built-in silencer in Lake Mead. This was the same gun Ron Rudin reported missing about six years before his death. When officials tested the gun in the forensics lab, the ammo matched the rounds found in Ron Rudin's skull. Police determined that the .22 was the murder weapon, and, with this new piece of evidence added to the other circumstantial clues they had, charged Margaret Rudin with the murder of her husband. However, Margaret left town before they indicted and arrested her, and she stayed out of sight for over two years.

Almost a year after the diver found the gun that allegedly killed Ron Rudin, police finally indicted Margaret Rudin.

Authorities finally apprehended Margaret Rudin in 1999. Someone who saw her picture and story on the T.V. show "America's Most Wanted" called and reported seeing her in a small town in Massachusetts.

Police used a pizza delivery person to help them capture Margaret. They borrowed the person's uniform and an empty pizza box, and barged in the house when her male companion opened the door. According to some reports, they found her cowering in the bathroom.

Margaret Rudin was born Margaret Lee Frost in Memphis, Tennessee on May 31, 1943. She said that she and her family never lived in one place for very long, and that she and her two sisters constantly changed schools.

"I didn't grow up any place. We were constantly moving, you know, like, I transferred schools 22 different times, um, before I graduated high school. I lived in 15 states in 15 years. I never had a hometown."

Margaret said that her father was strict and dominating, and that he rarely showed affection to her or her sisters.

Both Margaret and Ron were married four times before they met at the First Church of Religious Science in Las Vegas. They married on September 11, 1987.

Margaret's mother, Eloise Frost, stood behind her daughter throughout the entire trial. She never believed Margaret capable of murder.

"I want to live long enough to see Margaret pronounced innocent, because she is innocent."

Margaret Rudin's daughter, Kristina Mason firmly believed that her mother was innocent. She said her childhood was a good one, and that the mother with whom she grew up was not a murderer.

"She's just a wonderful person and I'm proud to say she's my mother."

The court sentenced Margaret Rudin in September 2001. Although she received life in a medium security facility, plus a year for planting the bugs in her husband's office, they also added that she would be eligible for parole in 2011. She began preparing, and petitioning, for her appeal, carefully heeding the filing deadlines.

80-year-old Eloise cried when Margaret was convicted, saying that now she may never see her daughter again.

Kristina Mason burst into tears.

"I'm so disappointed."

Ronald Rudin seemed to predict his own death, or at least his murder. Months before he went missing, he had his will changed, with specific instructions for investigators to follow in the event that he died under suspicious circumstances.

"In the event my death is caused by violent means [for example gunshot, knife or a violent automobile accident] extraordinary steps be taken in investigating the true cause of the death. Should said death be caused directly or indirectly by a beneficiary of my estate, said beneficiary shall be totally excluded from my estate and/or any trusts I may have in existence."

Although most of Nevada's case against Margaret was circumstantial, authorities say there were a few things that seemed suspicious to them from the beginning. First, Margaret herself admitted that her marriage to Ron was less than ideal. She told police that they often argued about her work schedule. Later, when authorities discovered that she had planted listening devices in Ron Rudin's home office, she also admitted that she suspected that Ron was having an affair, and upon eavesdropping on a phone conversation, discovered proof to back her suspicions.

Jimmy Vacarro, a Vegas detective, confirmed that the Las Vegas police believed without a doubt that Margaret Rudin was responsible for Ron's murder.

"We know there was this real rocky roller-coaster relationship between Margaret Rudin and her husband... [It took] Margaret two days to file a missing persons report and that she did so only after Ron's coworkers informed police first...Generally speaking, the spouse is missing, the wife's the one reporting it."

Second, officials say that Margaret waited a few days before reporting Ron missing, even though his employees at his real estate company were concerned and investigating as soon as he did not show up that Monday morning.

Margaret Rudin offered a logical explanation to her hesitation to bring in police. She said she thought little of it at first because they had another fight and he left angry, which was common for Ron. She also said that, aside from Ron being upset with her after an argument, he seemed like his usual self.

"He seemed ok. He does not seem upset. He had, had been a little peeved at me over the weekend because I had to work all the time... "Well, I thought nothing of it because, you know, maybe he did get peeved... and maybe he did decide to go out for awhile... maybe he did go to, you know... wherever."

Margaret made a point of mentioning her previous marriages in one of her interviews.

"I don't have a history of staying with somebody if I'm really unhappy. I have a history of divorcing... There was problems. He was a difficult person at times, but yes, I did love him..."

Margaret said Ron also drank quite a bit after just a few months of marriage. However, she told reporters that she was not mad about the alcohol or the other women, even when Su Lyles, a close friend and a former employee of Mr. Rudin's, testified that in the fall of 1993, their relationship became more intimate. At least twice, she said, they had discussed their feelings for each other over the telephone during calls made from his office.

"You know why? It is because 99 percent of the men that I have ever had in my life had affairs. Ninety percent of men do, you might as well expect it."

Margaret admitted that, although the affairs wounded her, she loved her husband and desperately wanted to work out things with him.

Police grew even more suspicious when they discovered that Margaret hired a man named Augustine Lovato to help her remove some dirty carpet and furniture from the master bedroom. She then renovated the bedroom she shared with her husband into an office while Ron was still missing.

Lovato testified that the mattress and carpet he removed from the Rudin's home had suspicious brown stains on it and a strong odor that alarmed him.

"It didn't seem right, him still being missing and me turning their master bedroom into an office and then those splatters on that picture. Like I got the heebie-jeebies."

Lovato also claimed that he heard a strange sound in the bathtub in the master bathroom. He said that, upon inspection, it looked about the same color and consistency as the stains on the mattress and carpet he removed.

The same day he moved the allegedly bloodstained items from the Rudin's bedroom, Margaret Rudin asked Lovato to mail a package addressed to her mother. Lovato claimed that he forgot to mail the package, and ultimately turned it over to the police. After obtaining a search warrant, police opened the package and discovered several personal items inside, including a postcard from Israel signed "Love, Yehuda," a photo of Yehuda Sharon, the man with whom police suspected that Margaret Rudin was having an affair, and a handwritten letter from Rudin to her mother containing the message, "Please hold on to my Ye."

Attorneys discovered later that Lovato reported all these mysterious findings after Ron Rudin's other trustees announced their reward for information about Ron's disappearance. However, Lovato argued that he cooperated with police before anyone told him there was a reward, which Ron's trustees did grant him.

The most suspicious thing that Margaret Rudin did, according to police, was going on the run before the state served her with her indictment. Investigators believed that, if Margaret were innocent, she would not have fled. However, Margaret says that she ran out of fear, not guilt.

"[I ran] because I was afraid of being found by Ron's shadowy business associates... It was difficult. I was always looking over my shoulder. I was always afraid, I was afraid of who stood to gain the most, you know, from Ron's murder."

During the trial, the state also used the testimony of almost 70 witnesses, including Yehuda Sharon and Margaret's sister, Donna Cantrell. Prosecutors granted Yehuda Sharon total immunity in exchange for his testimony against Margaret Rudin. However, when he took the stand, he not only had little to say regarding Margaret's guilt, he denied aiding her in disposing of Ron Rudin's remains. He told the court that he rented a van, planning to make a trip from Vegas to California for his business on the night in question. However, he said that he only made it half way there and then turned around due to unexpected weather conditions. Furthermore, his destination was the opposite direction from the place where officials found Ron Rudin's remains. Once the prosecution determined that Margaret's friend, Yehuda Sharon, was likely not an accomplice to Ron's murder, no other suspects were detained or questions, and most people assumed that Margaret had somehow dismembered her husband's body, put it in the heavy steamer trunk and hauled it out to the desert all by herself.

Cantrell testified that she was aware of her sister's marital problems. She said that Margaret had spoken to her many times about Ron's drinking and her suspicions about his involvement with other women. She made comments on Rudin's restless desire to get away from Ron.

"I said, 'I thought you were going to divorce him,' and she said, 'He's not in very good health. He can't even walk without being out of breath, and I think I'll wait.' [Margaret told me] to tell [police] that she and Ron were getting along better than ever. And that the girlfriend wasn't an issue. [I don't] think that this statement would have been true."

Despite the authorities' strong belief that she murdered her husband, Margaret Rudin maintained her innocents. In interviews after the trial and her conviction, she states repeatedly that she loved her husband and could never kill him. She suggested that there might be another motive for her husband's murder.

"Nobody knows the whole Ron. That's the part that worries me. Maybe there's something that was going on with a business or a personal deal."

Margaret also suspected that someone knew more than they told detectives.

"I think that there are people that know things. I think that there are people who haven't come forth before. Maybe they didn't know how, maybe they were afraid, maybe they were intimidated."

Margaret Rudin's trial was rocky from the beginning. One of her defense attorneys, Michael Amador, started with an opening statement, which consisted of nothing but a long, irrelevant, self-based speech.

"This is a great day, in a lot of different ways. Some days are difficult; some days we hear bad news or we go through a difficult time, but every day, every day, depending on how you look at it, with a few exceptions, can be a celebration.

This is a great today for me. This is a culmination of a career. The people in this case, we are not strangers; we know each other. Chris and

I were sworn in as deputy DAs the same day. And I congratulate Chris on a presentation that was organized and well thought out, the best money can buy. It was really good.

If you want to know an opinion about me, I guarantee you'll find some, different ones from different people. Not many people know me. I have few close friends, like Ronald Rudin had few close friends.

I could be a wonderful, caring father, coaching soccer, helping kids with their homework, which I did the first time I got married when they were young.

Then another day, I might scream at someone, yell at them for-I don't know-for asking me some question, because I was too busy and I was thinking of something else.

The difficulty I have at times is communicating to people. I have to look at it and talk to other people and they will bring me back down to earth and say, Mike, what are you trying to say? What are you trying to get across?"

Amador also made a strange, challenging statement.

"During the course of the trial, there may be objections and things like that. Don't worry about it."

Judge Joseph Bonaventure cut off Amador's speech.

"I don't know what that means: Don't worry about objections. We have to do other things. I have no idea what that means. If there's an objection, I'm either going to overrule it or sustain it and that's the law... I keep saying this-and I let you get away with a lot, Mr. Amador-but the purpose for an opening statement is just to indicate what the evidence is going to tend to show and not go into your personal beliefs and your passion and soccer dad and yelling at the staff and whether you were a green lawyer and know all the cops and used to be a D.A. and you communicate differently. I never heard that in [an] opening statement in my life."

During the opening statements, the State quoted a portion of Margaret Rudin's diary.

"My life has always been unique, exciting, full of change, challenges and stimulus and full of interesting casts of characters and that is okay.

It just is, and I accept that for my past, but I know that, by programming my mind, I can now redirect any future stage plays and pick my own screen play and cast, because I am the producer, director and star of any and all new plays on my stage called life.

I've always vaguely known these facts and lived my life accordingly, but I never realized what control-I never realized what control I could have over every segment of this one time stage production called "Margaret's Life.""

Amador did a curious thing at the trial. He employed a makeup artist from a professional modeling agency and paid almost $500 an hour, out of his own pocket, to make Margaret appear worn, delicate, and tired.

Amador got under Judge Bonaventure's skin by repeatedly being late to appear in court, questionable forms he submitted, and his cell phone, which he never turned off or down during the trial. Rumors eventually spread that Amador was using drugs, drinking and partying all night long when he had to be in court early the next morning.

Rumors circulated that Amador was also behaving inappropriately with Margaret Rudin's belongings and private, confidential information. Amador hired a new office assistant named Annie Jackson during the proceedings for the Rudin trial. She revealed information regarding some of the rumors about Amador.

"There is no other way to say the following: when Mr. Amador told the court that he did not have any book or movie contracts, he was lying. Michael Amador does have book contracts and movie contracts regarding the Margaret Rudin case. When we returned to the office after Mr. Amador made those false representations to the court, he asked me to grab all of the contracts so that he could put them in his little safe in the back closet. He told me, "I don't want anyone to find out that I have these, then I'm sure they'll be investigating and looking for these."

Margaret asked early on for an even amount of participation from her attorneys. She asked that Thomas Pitaro take a more active role in the proceedings, because she did not believe that Michael Amador was properly prepared.

"We haven't even subpoenaed my witnesses yet. And I'm getting so nervous. I mean, I'm getting panicky."

Pitaro agreed after warning the judge that, although he would do his best, he was uncertain if he would be able to uphold that bargain throughout the entire trial.

Throughout all the chaos in the Rudin trial, one juror believed Margaret's side of the story. During the first couple of days of deliberation, she held fast to her opinion that Margaret did not kill Ron. However, hours before the foreperson read the jury's verdict, juror #11 changed her vote. She was distraught, wiping her eyes with a napkin. She hesitated before replying with a hushed "Yes" when the court asked her if the verdict was, in fact, hers, too.

Even though the verdict was ultimately unanimous, the juror cried as she apologized to Rudin when the foreperson read the jury's verdict.

During the time before she opted to vote Margaret Rudin guilty, juror #11 faced allegations from her peers of choosing not to join the deliberation efforts, lying, and calling one of the jury substitutes with her concerns about the case. Amador said he thought the juror was possibly "brow-beaten" into changing her vote.

Foreperson for the Rudin case's jury, Ronald Vest, said that no one "twisted her arm."

"We didn't bribe her or threaten her. She came to this on her own."

Vest believed that Rudin's was an open and shut case.

"Rudin's guilt was clear early on. [The defense's case was] a waste of time... [Amador was] bordering on incompetent... [The guilty verdict was a] slam dunk with a stepladder... I didn't buy any of it. I don't think any of us bought any of the defense case. The mountain of evidence had 11 of the jurors ready to convict as early as Thursday, but one person from the beginning did not see it that way... juror #11 seemed so bent on acquitting Rudin that [I] began to wonder if she had been bribed or threatened or simply wanted attention. [I] confronted her about [my] suspicions, and she denied them. There was a little bit of swearing. It was fast and furious but we hashed it out."

Vest admitted that he had had to request substitutes on a few occasions, because his special needs students were struggling in class without him. He believed that, had he not been there, they would not have been able to replace him.

"Six substitutes, three of which said they would never come back and one who just sat at the desk shaking like he was scared... my principal said, Well, maybe there's some reason why you need to be on this jury."

The judge in the Rudin trial met with the hesitant juror privately, in his chambers, to address her contact, and discussion about case-related information, with an alternate juror. Whenever Margaret Rudin's defense team broached the subject, the court dismissed it, stating that it had little impact on the outcome of the trial.

Margaret Rudin's conviction shocked Amador. He spoke with disdain about the prosecutors. He could not believe that the prosecutors successfully sold their case.

"If you have any understanding of psychology, history, or criminology, women don't do that, men do," said Amador. "That kind of mutilation is done by men over money or, in rare cases, serial killers. Women don't even order stuff like that—they want it clean... [The prosecutors] make me sick... I don't know how it is that right-thinking people can find someone guilty with no evidence."

Rudin had requested a mistrial due to Amador's antics and all the dissention with the jury. Pitaro led the defense team at the motion, hoping to prove that Amador was ill prepared for the case and not behaving with appropriate competence as an attorney.

"The fundamental problem that we have is this case is not ready to go to trial. For whatever reason it's not ready, it's not ready. That's obvious to any observer of this case, that for the first two weeks this is not the way you try cases and this is not the way you try murder cases. And what we are putting on in front of the world is a farce, and that disturbs me as an attorney. [T]his has become a sham, a farce and a mockery."

The State expressed similar concerns.

"Already we have an appellate issue now, should they have hired a forensic accountant. And I mean they came into this thing hiring their experts two weeks before the trial and they didn't start looking at the evidence until the day of trial. Two days into it, we still don't have reports back for most of them... Mr. Pitaro is coming in now, he's going to try to read the stuff and catch up. He already feels there's certain things that should have happened that didn't happen. All I can say is we're really uncomfortable with the record here."

The district court, however, was hesitant to declare a mistrial because of the double jeopardy laws. As it turned out, those did not apply in Margaret Rudin's case.

Amador stood with Margaret Rudin and the rest of her defense team during the motion for mistrial. However, when the prosecutors submitted documentation regarding his ineffectiveness, he contradicted himself.

"Nobody worked harder or spent more time before or during the Rudin trial nor knew the case better than I... [I] spend many hours on the case, from the time [I] took it in August of 2000 and [my] vacation in November 2000... [I] filed at least 24 motions and investigated all major witnesses in the case and organized their files prior to the vacation."

The defense also argued that improper communication took place between the judge, juror 11 and the alternate, which tainted the jury. According to the alternate, juror 11 called the alternate, saying she was upset because she was the only person in favor of a not guilty verdict and because she had gotten into an altercation with the staff person at a restaurant during a recess. After questioning the alternate and the juror in the presence of the State and the defense, the district court denied Rudin's motion for a mistrial. The district court also chose not to replace the juror. They concluded that neither the jury nor Rudin's case were compromised.

The court removed Amador from Margaret Rudin's case, but rejected her request for a mistrial. The judge almost immediately disregarded Margaret's mistrial motion.

"[Rudin] failed to present any specific argument to support a determination that she has been prejudiced. [The] affidavits are legally insufficient, as conclusions, rumors, beliefs, and opinions are not sufficient to form a basis for a new trial... As to Mr. Amador's personal antics which the defense seems to harp upon as tantalizing tidbits, this court feels it is not honorable to kick a man when he is down as the record speaks for itself. Rudin, at taxpayer expense, also had at her side criminal defense attorneys Thomas Pitaro and John Momot."

Bonaventure was biased, blunt, and cold at Margaret's sentencing hearing, just as he was throughout the entire trial.

"You're going to be locked away in the cold confines of your prison cell, never to be heard from again."

Although she received life in a medium security facility, plus a year for planting the bugs in her husband's office, they also added that she would be eligible for parole in 2011. She began preparing, and petitioning, for her appeal, carefully heeding the filing deadlines.

The appeals court believed that one of Margaret Rudin's former attorneys, Dayvid Figler, was responsible for her initial petitions for appeal. Figler denied any wrongdoing, and said that, although he was not at fault, she did deserve a shot at a new trial.

"I didn't screw up her trial. I didn't screw up her appeal. The court was giving extra time to get this very burdensome case before it. Everyone was operating under the assumption that she had more time to file the post-conviction appeal."

Figler called Rudin's appeal a "very complicated, burdensome, voluminous case" and said that after he took it on, the trial judge granted him extra time because the case was so complex.

Christopher Oram, the lawyer who represented Margaret Rudin during her recent appeal for a new trial, was thrilled with the opportunity.

"She is absolutely innocent. We've been working to prove it for a long time. I'm trying to reverse 10 years of complex litigation that was very unfair... I believe in her innocence. I'm ready to fight, and I wish they would stop playing their games. In the end, get in the ring and fight."

The Ninth Circuit Court of Appeals said that a technicality should not hinder Margaret Rudin's attempt to prove that a lawyer at her original trial ineffectually proved her case. Judge Mary Murguia believed that Figler did not serve Margaret to the best of his ability.

"While Figler regularly attended the court's status hearings, he appears to have done nothing else in support of his client's request for post-conviction relief. [Figler had the case for 645 days] and during that time, [he] had filed nothing in either state or federal court."

In 2007, Oram filed the first and only petition for post-conviction relief, according to Murguia.

Sally Loehrer, a district judge, ruled in 2008 that Michael Amador's performance did constitute as ineffectual in her original trial, and as a result, Margaret Rudin was entitled to a new trial.

"[It was a] case laced with intrigue and spins and loops involving a cast of characters and witnesses [that seemed to have] a lot of ulterior motives."

However, two years later, the Supreme Court overruled, stating that there was not enough evidence to sustain the order.

The Ninth Circuit Court reviewed all the evidence from the original trial, as well as Margaret Rudin's complaints, and her defense team's strategies. They do not believe that all defense attorneys adequately represent their clients just because they participate in every aspect of the trial. They made mention of evidence that was not previously mentioned.

"Sometime during the trial, the defense team located the person who sold the trunk to Rudin and established that it was not a large humpback trunk, but one that was much too small to fit a corpse inside. The defense also located Barbara Orcutt, who indicated that Rudin was indeed concerned about Ron's disappearance and had asked her right after his disappearance to organize a search in the Mt. Charleston area, where she believed Ron might have been. The State apparently had this information, but did not share it with the defense. It is unrealistic to think that the jurors could have put out of their minds all the evidence and adverse events, including the continual admonishment of defense counsel by the district court judge; the bizarre opening statement; the constant continuances and delays throughout the trial, which I am sure were held against the defense; and the belated presentation of important evidence. These harmful events resulted from Amador's conflict of interest and lack of preparation and now require reversal of this case... The evidence certainly indicated that Amador secured media rights while representing Rudin, which was a violation of the Nevada Rules of Professional Conduct.9...Amador was clearly more interested in obtaining information for his book and getting media attention than in developing Rudin's defense."

They also noted the testimony from Annie Jackson, Amador's assistant, and found new information there, as well. Jackson claimed that Amador did not turn over several of Rudin's files, containing diaries, witness statements, and pictures, to the public defender's office because he thought he might need the information in the future.

"I believe there is sufficient evidence in the record, without the necessity of post-trial proceedings, to establish that the defense was totally unprepared to try this case and that Amador had a substantial conflict of interest with his client. This was prejudicial to Rudin, and the result reached was unreliable."

Margaret appeals to the public in a letter she wrote from the Florence McClure Women's Correctional Center.

"The new trial I won [on] March 10, 2015, in the Ninth Circuit Court of Appeals has been blocked by the new NV Attorney General. Next week, their writ to the U.S. Supreme court will be filed."

She explains that, if her case lands in the 99% that skip review this session, it will return to the Ninth Circuit. Since they have already voted in her favor before, she hopes that once again, the NCCA will find her worthy of a new trial, and that this time their decision will be permanent. She maintains her innocence, and she continues to push for her appeal, and her opportunity to have her side of the story told.

CHRISTA PIKE

Christa Gail Pike, born 10 March 1976, currently sits on Tennessee's death row for the murder of Colleen Slemmer, 19, on 12 January 1995. The murder occurred when Pike was 18 years old. Pike and her then-boyfriend Tadaryl Shipp who was 17 at the time of the murder were convicted of Slemmer's murder and conspiracy to commit murder. Another friend of the defendants and the victim, Shadolla Peterson, also 18 at the time, was convicted as an accessory after the fact and given six years' probation after turning informant. Pike was sentenced to death by electrocution in 1996 and, at the time, she had the distinction of being the youngest woman ever to be sentenced to death, in any state and only the second women given the death penalty in Tennessee.

Early Life

Pike's life reads like a primer for depraved murderers. As a small child, Pike did not enjoy a healthy and supportive bond with her mother, Carissa Hansen, a licensed nurse, allegedly because of her premature birth. Whereas thousands of children are born prematurely and do not resort to criminal behavior Pike's birth was presented as evidence of one possible origin of her poor and troubled behavior. Pike's maternal grandmother was verbally abusive and Pike was raised by her alcoholic and abusive paternal grandmother until the latter's death in 1988 when Pike was 12; after which Pike attempted suicide by overdosing. She was then shuttled back and forth between her divorced parents' homes. In 1989, Pike was kicked out of her father's house for the second and final time due to her unruliness and the alleged sexual abuse of her father's then-two-year old daughter with his second wife.

Prior to the murder, experts assert that there were myriad indications that Pike was seriously disturbed; however, nobody who may have suspected this sought help for the increasingly disobedient and incorrigible young lady. According to Pike's mother, she was problematic since the age of eight and the two of them had a contentious relationship due to Pike's fluctuating and troubling behavior. Her mother asserted that by age nine Pike was growing marijuana in pots at their home and had been permitted to have a live-in boyfriend at age 14. At one point—in an effort to improve their relationship—Hansen suggested that she and Pike smoke marijuana together. Hansen mistakenly believed that cultivating a friendship with her daughter would cultivate the necessary bond Pike had been lacking her entire life. At one point, one of her mother's boyfriends whipped Pike with a belt which prompted her to wield a butcher knife against him before he was subsequently arrested. Hansen also admitted that Pike had repeatedly lied to and stolen from her. In several interviews with Hansen throughout Pike's trial and seemingly endless appeals, she admitted repeatedly that she was a terrible mother and should have spent more time with her daughter.

Pike's aunt, Carrie Ross, provided insight into Pike's upbringing when she testified that she disallowed her own children from associating with Pike because she lived in a filthy house that had zero ground rules and that Pike was a pathological liar of whom she was somewhat afraid. She also admitted that there was a history of substance abuse in Pike's family. Ross also stated that on the few occasions that Pike actually visited her she behaved like a little girl and engaged in Barbie and dress-up play with her eleven-year-old cousin. Further, there were some allegations that Pike may have been sexually abused but these were neither confirmed nor denied.

Pike's father, Glenn Pike testified that he did, in fact, kick his daughter out of his house multiple times; the last time being in 1989 after the aforementioned allegations that Pike sexually abused her two-year old half-sister. He admitted that he had signed adoption papers for Pike prior to her 18th birthday and that during the times she resided with him she was manipulative, disobedient, and dishonest.

After dropping out of high school, Pike began Job Corps classes in computer programming. Job Corps is a government-based organization that provides occupational and vocational training to underprivileged and troubled teens. It was at the now-defunct Job Corps center in Knoxville where she met Shipp, Slemmer, and Peterson. While Job Corps seeks to promote prosocial behavior and foster a strong desire among its participants to learn a vocation and secure a more promising future than might have been previously the case, this program is also known to cultivate criminal activity, likely due to the association among its participants; many of whom already had problematic behavior.

Evidence of Premeditation

On 11 January 1995, the day before the actual homicide, Pike told friend and co-Job Corps student Kim Iloilo that she was planning to kill Slemmer because she "just felt mean that day." Iloilo discounted Pike's statement as nothing more than merely talk; however, the following evening at approximately 8:00 p.m. Iloilo witnessed Pike, Shipp, Peterson, and Slemmer leaving the Job Corps center. When Iloilo saw Pike, Shipp, and Peterson returning at approximately 10:15 p.m. without Slemmer she, again, thought nothing of it. Even when Pike visited Iloilo's dorm room at 11:00 p.m. that night and confessed to killing Slemmer—as well as showing Iloilo what Pike identified as a piece of Slemmer's skull—Iloilo still failed to tell anyone. Later, at Pike's trial, Iloilo testified that while Pike was iterating the events of the murder she was oddly smiling, singing, and dancing around the room. The following morning Iloilo asked Pike what she was going to do with the piece of skull. Pike nonchalantly replied that she had it in her pocket and was, in fact, eating breakfast with it.

Pike also told another student, Stephanie Wilson, a similar account the following day and proudly described the brown spots on her shoes as blood. Not unlike Iloilo, Wilson failed to immediately report anything.

The Crime Scene

On 13 January, officers from the University of Tennessee and Knoxville Police Departments were dispatched to greenhouses on the University's agricultural campus in Tyson Park where a University grounds department employee reported finding, at approximately 8:05 a.m., what he assumed to be a dead animal. The gruesome discovery was a corpse that turned out to be Colleen Slemmer. She was naked from the waist up; her throat was cut; her head had been bludgeoned; and she had various cuts all over her arms, throat, and torso—including a pentagram that had been carved into her chest. Officer John Terry Johnson who testified at Pike's trial described Slemmer's body as so badly beaten that she was unrecognizable as a human being. He also stated that he thought he was looking at her face when, in reality,

Slemmer was lying face-down in the dirt and debris where Pike, Shipp, and Peterson had left her.

There was additional evidence and testimony that the crime scene encompassed an area that measured 100 feet long by 60 feet wide; an astounding 6,000 square feet in area. Despite the area being muddy and wet there was ample evidence of a physical struggle with trampled bushes, a considerable amount of blood, body drag marks, and hand and knee prints. Thirty feet from Slemmer's body was a large pool of blood which suggested that Slemmer was attacked in one area and then dragged to where her body was later found. Slemmer's shirt and bra were also discovered at the crime scene, as well as a bloody rag that Pike admitted to tying over Slemmer's mouth at one point to keep her from screaming.

Disturbingly, University of Tennessee police officer Harold James Underwood, Jr., who was the officer assigned to secure the crime scene, testified at trial that Pike and a few other females came to the scene between four and five p.m. the day of the discovery and before Pike was even considered to be a suspect. Underwood stated that Pike had asked why the wooded area was marked off, who the victim was, and whether police had any leads as to who the suspect or suspects were. He particularly recalled Pike's odd behavior—moving around a lot while giggling amusedly—and that she wore a necklace in the shape of a pentagram. The following day, during briefing when informed that the victim had a pentagram carved into her chest, Underwood reported Pike's behavior and necklace to his supervisors.

Autopsy and Findings

During Slemmer's autopsy, the medical examiner, Dr. Sandra Elkins, had to identify the victim's body from dental records because her head was so bludgeoned that she was unrecognizable. After cleaning up Slemmer's body which was clad only in jeans, socks, and shoes, and covered with dirt and twigs, Dr. Elkins began cataloging Slemmer's wounds. Due to the sheer number of wounds on her back, arms, abdomen, and chest, and the fact that following department policy which stated that each individual wound be assigned a letter of the alphabet, when Dr. Elkins reached double letters she, instead, individually catalogued only the most serious wounds and that there were innumerable other superficial and defensive wounds. Among the most serious cuts was a six-inch gaping wound across Slemmer's throat that was deep enough to penetrate the fat and muscles in her neck as well as the aforementioned pentagram. Additional injuries included fresh bruising which Dr. Elkins asserted was consistent with crawling.

Cause of death was ultimately attributed to blunt force trauma to the head. Dr. Elkins surmised that Slemmer's head was hit with the asphalt at least four times—two to the left side, one over the right eye, and one to the nose—which collectively resulted in multiple and extensive skull fractures. One of these blows was to the left side of Slemmer's head—which, according to Dr. Elkins, occurred with the right side of the victim's head against a firm surface. This blow only fractured her skull but also imbedded a portion of Slemmer's skull into her head and contained black particles from the piece of asphalt determined to be the murder weapon.

Even more tragic was Dr. Elkins' findings that none of Slemmer's other wounds would have rendered her unconscious and evidence of active blood flow around the wounds and blood in her sinus cavity indicated that Slemmer was alive during the severe torture she suffered before being killed.

Arrest and Confession

The police quickly connected Pike to the homicide thanks to the piece of Slemmer's skull discovered in Pike's jacket pocket. Pike had left this jacket hanging on the back of a chair in Job Corps Orientation Specialist Robert A. Pollock's office on 13 January after meeting with him about a misplaced ID card. Pike's jacket remained in Pollock's office from 4:00 p.m. on 13 January until 7:30 a.m. on 17 January. After learning over the weekend that Pike was a suspect in Slemmer's murder investigation, Pollock immediately gave the jacket to William Hudson, the Job Corps' safety and security captain who turned it over to Knoxville Police Department Officer Arthur Bohanan. At trial, Bohanan would testify that he found a small piece of bone in one of the pockets and presented it to Dr. Murray Marks, a University of Tennessee forensic anthropologist who was reconstructing Slemmer's decapitated skull and the piece in Pike's jacket pocket fit perfectly into an area where a portion of her skull was missing at the time of the victim's discovery.

When confronted with this evidence and subsequently arrested, Pike waived her *Miranda* protections and confessed to the murder and permitted officers to search her dorm room where the blood-soaked jeans she wore the previous night were found. Additionally, Pike led officers to a trash can at a nearby Texaco station on Cumberland Avenue where she had disposed of Slemmer's ID and a pair of gloves Pike had been wearing at the time of the homicide.

Pike's transcribed confession was 46 pages long.

In it, Pike admitted that there was animosity between Slemmer and her because Pike was convinced that Slemmer was a rival for the affections of her boyfriend, Shipp, and that Slemmer was trying to get Pike kicked out of the Job Corps program so she could have Shipp for herself. Pike also claimed that she had awakened one night to find Slemmer standing above her with a box cutter; however, there is no evidence of this allegation. Instead, Slemmer had repeatedly called her mother, May Martinez, to tell her she was afraid of Pike who she had awakened to find in her room and that she wanted to come home; to which Slemmer's mother said that she couldn't because she had signed a contract. Pike stated that she had only planned to fight Slemmer to stop her from running her mouth. On that fateful night of 12 January, Pike, Slemmer, Shipp, and Peterson signed the Job Corps logbook as they were leaving for an outing Slemmer believed was to smoke marijuana en route to a video store so that Pike and she could try to work out their problems.

When the group entered a tunnel at the edge of Tyson Park, Slemmer likely felt that something was not quite right and proceeded to ask Pike where they were going and whether there was, in fact, any marijuana. These questions irritated Pike who began the brutal assault shortly thereafter after they had gone deeply enough into the woods so that nobody could hear them that led to Slemmer's murder.

Pike confessed to initially slamming Slemmer's head into her knee and then throwing her to the ground where Pike continually punched, kicked, and slammed Slemmer's head into the concrete, screaming, "the bi*ch won't die" and that she wanted "to see [Slemmer's] brains flow." According to witnesses Shipp and Peterson, as Slemmer continued to plead with Pike to stop, Pike got angrier and more brutal. Slemmer offered to return to her Florida home, leave her belongings at the Job Corps center, and not tell anyone what happened; however, Pike became more enraged and yelled at Slemmer to be quiet because "it was harder to hurt someone who was talking to you."

In addition to the savage beating, Slemmer had been cut innumerable times with a box cutter and a mini meat cleaver (that Pike had allegedly borrowed from another Job Corps student) to her torso, arms, face, and back including having had her throat slit six times prior to the fatal blow that resulted from having her head crushed by a piece of asphalt. There was also a pentagram carved into Slemmer's chest; however, Pike asserted that Shipp had done that. Pike also confessed to "just watching Slemmer bleed" when the victim got up and tried to run away. Pike admitted to cutting Slemmer's back: "the big long cut."

After the murder, Pike stated that she and Shipp washed their hands and shoes in a nearby mud puddle to conceal the blood, dumped the box cutter, and Pike returned the meat cleaver to the person from which she borrowed it. This person has never been identified.

The physical evidence and co-defendant testimony suggested that the assault and murder lasted from 30 minutes to an hour and consisted of Slemmer repeatedly trying to get up and run away but was prevented from doing so by the co-defendants who also, as Pike testified, contributed to the physical assault by throwing rocks at Slemmer's head and holding her down so she couldn't run away. Later, Pike would testify that she heard voices in her head overriding Slemmer's continual screaming, telling her that she needed to prevent Slemmer from filing charges against her for attempted murder. Pike also admitted that at one point she thought she had heard a noise and went to investigate it to ensure that they were alone, as well as alleging that during the assault she heard Slemmer breathing in blood and jerking but did not let this assuage her anger as Pike continued her savagery.

Even more troublesome, a police video recorded after Pike's confession shows Pike smiling and providing extensive details about the crime at the crime scene, oftentimes mimicking her actions that evening. Many have said that her demeanor on the recording was eerily similar to that of a little girl who was excited and happy that she had experienced the best day of her life and had no problem talking about the events that transpired, the heinousness of her actions, and how she felt about it all.

The facts of the homicide are not nor have they ever been in dispute, thanks to an abundance of evidence. Pike's confession, and witness testimony at the trial.

Pre-Trial Examination

Prior to her trial, Pike was given a battery of assessment tests and examined by numerous psychiatrists including clinical psychologist Dr. Eric Engum who found her to be extremely bright as evidenced by an I.Q. of 111—in the 77th percentile of the general population—which he believed to be remarkable given her difficult childhood and lack of formal schooling beyond the ninth grade. Dr. Engum also found that

Pike had excellent reasoning, problem solving, language, and analytic skills, and was also quite adept at paying attention, sustaining concentration, and sequencing information. Dr. Engum concluded that Pike was legally sane and had no brain damage which has frequently been demonstrated to cause violent behavior in some individuals.

Of particular interest was that Pike was found to be marijuana- and inhalant-dependent and also diagnosed with borderline personality disorder. Whereas there are some similarities between borderline personality disorder and antisocial personality disorder such as impulsivity, irritability, aggression, and a self-image that fluctuates between self-aggrandizement and despair, there are several differences. Individuals with borderline personality disorder differ from those with antisocial behavior in that the former—which primarily affects females—is characterized by a lack of remorse, self-destructiveness, black-and-white thinking, alcohol and/or drug use or abuse, unstable relationships characterized by fear of abandonment and extreme swings between love and hate, difficulty in achieving academic and vocational goals, and are more likely to have been sexually abused; while the latter—which affects disproportionately more males—is characterized by a lack of affect and remorse, emptiness, and an ultimate goal of self-preservation.

Pike demonstrated all of the aforementioned characteristics of borderline personality disorder which makes it easier—but not justifiably so—to comprehend how her intense jealousy of Slemmer and fear of losing Shipp made her commit her atrocious acts. In addition to her fear of abandonment, Pike also abused drugs, was likely sexually abused, had contentious relationships, and displayed zero remorse. Dr. Engum surmised that Pike did not act with premeditation or deliberation in Slemmer's murder but, instead, in a manner that was consistent with borderline personality disorder. More simply, Pike had lost control. However, on cross-examination Dr. Engum admitted that Pike's deliberate luring of Slemmer, that she carved a pentagram in the victim's chest, that she brought weapons with her, and that she bashed Slemmer's head into the concrete does, in fact, constitute deliberateness.

That Pike was overjoyed and singing in Iloilo's room describing the murder while dancing around with the portion of Slemmer's skull Pike had taken as a trophy further supported Dr. Engum's diagnosis of borderline personality disorder because she had eliminated who she perceived was in competition for her boyfriend, Shipp, and, therefore, could continue her relationship with him. When questioned about the piece of skull Pike had taken, Dr. Engum said that Pike had no identity and her actions of taking and displaying the skull was a way to get recognition, no matter how misleading and distorted said recognition might be. In fact, after her conviction and sentencing Pike wrote a letter to Shipp which was intercepted by jail personnel that stated that even though she tried to be "nice" to Slemmer by bashing in her head instead of letting her bleed to death she was still sentenced to "fry."

The Trial

There was an abundance of evidence presented at the trial. Physical evidence consisted of crime scene photographs, autopsy reports, bloody clothing, and the piece of Slemmer's skull Pike had taken as a trophy. With respect to this skull piece, Dr. Elkins presented Slemmer's decapitated skull that was reconstructed by Dr. Marks to explain the victim's injuries. The skull presented at trial was complete except for a portion that was missing on the left side of Slemmer's skull. Dr. Elkins demonstrated that the piece of skull found in Pike's jacket fit perfectly into this spot, much to the chagrin of Slemmer's mother who, in a taped interview, stated that Pike was oftentimes giggling and passing notes to her mother and defense attorney during the trial, not unlike an immature middle-schooler.

At the trial, the State introduced photographs taken of Pike and Shipp at the Knoxville Police Department in which both were wearing pentagram necklaces similar to the shape carved into Slemmer's chest. It was presented that both Pike and Shipp dabbled in devil worshiping and other forms of the occult and that Slemmer was a sacrifice for the next day, Friday the 13th. Despite the presence of some type of satanic elements in Slemmer's murder, Dr. William Bernet, Vanderbilt University's psychiatric hospital medical director, testified that the evidence was that of "an adolescent dabbling in Satanism." He further concluded that the concept of collective aggression—or mob mentality—in which a group of people become stimulated and subsequently engage in some type of violent behavior was most assuredly at play in the events leading to Slemmer's death. However, Dr. Bernet ultimately stated that he did not have enough evidence to definitively surmise whether Pike had acted with premeditation or intent when she lured and murdered Slemmer.

Pike was ultimately convicted of first-degree murder and conspiracy to commit first-degree murder after a mere two-and-a-half hours of jury deliberation. The fact that the jury returned guilty verdicts for first-degree murder—and did it so quickly—demonstrate that jurors were convinced that Pike had the requisite mens rea, or mental capacity, to warrant a first-degree murder charge: premeditation and deliberation. Amidst the overwhelming evidence and utter lack of remorse for her actions Pike was sentenced to death by electrocution (Tennessee has since adopted lethal injection for executions but has the prerogative to utilize electrocution if the lethal injection drugs cannot be obtained). Shipp was sentenced to life without parole because his age at the time of the murder was too young to warrant capital punishment and Peterson turned informant and was given six years' probation for her testimony.

Pike's conviction was upheld by the Court of Criminal Appeals and the United States Supreme Court denied certiorari.

Post-Conviction

While incarcerated, Pike demonstrated more evidence of her depravity. In 2001 she tried to murder fellow inmate Patricia Jones by strangling her with a shoelace. Pike alleges that Jones repeatedly tortured her by calling her "fried chicken" and making various demeaning sounds as an affront to what Jones said was the sound that Pike would make when she was electrocuted. The final straw was when Jones physically threatened Pike's friend, fellow devil worshiper Natasha Cornet. Pike said that she jumped atop Jones and choked her with a shoelace so that the much larger and heavier Jones would get off of Cornet. By the time prison guards reached them, Jones was unconscious.

Pike was subsequently convicted of attempted murder despite her prior death sentence because any offense committed while an individual is incarcerated must be adjudicated. During this time, neurology specialist Dr. Jonathan Henry Pincus began investigating Pike's brain to glean some type of knowledge as to why Pike behaved and continued to act violently the way she did when she assaulted Jones. He asserted that every killer he has ever examined share three commonalities: brain damage, a history of abuse, and mental illness. Dr. Pincus alleged that Pike did, in fact, possess all three features and demonstrates all of the requisite features common to serial killers. There is much consensus among professionals that Pike would likely have been a serial killer had she not been caught the first time.

He also testified at Pike's attempted murder trial that her brain's frontal lobes are not "put together properly"; largely due, he claimed, to the fact that Pike's mother drank while she was pregnant with Pike despite denial of this by Pike's mother. It was also brought up that as a child Pike played at the slaughterhouse where her grandfather worked and that she was frequently subjected to pornography and horror movies on the home television screen. He asserted that all of these factors provide insight into how an 18-year old girl could act with such depravity as was the case when Pike murdered Slemmer.

However, the original trial judge, Mary Beth Leibowitz, stated that Pincus' "findings" of brain damage was curious as the defense expert at Pike's original trial who was trying to spare her the death penalty failed to find such evidence.

Forensic psychiatrist William Kenner testified that Pike had suffered from undiagnosed bipolar disorder, the symptoms of which were evident from the time Pike was a "sleepless, talkative adolescent" and likened her to an automobile with cruise control set at 120 miles per hour. Pike's post-conviction defense team alleged that this non-diagnosis justified her requesting a new trial.

In 2002 Pike sought to have her appeal legally stopped and to proceed with her execution. In June of that year Judge Leibowitz granted Pike's request and scheduled an execution date of 19 August 2002. However, a few days later Pike changed her mind and the Tennessee Court of Appeals subsequently stayed her execution. In October 2005, Pike's death sentence was affirmed; however, no execution date has been set at this time.

Pike was again in court in 2007 when her defense team headed by Donald E. Dawson asserted sought a new trial, alleging ineffective assistance of counsel in that her trial defense team failed to introduce evidence supporting Pike's alleged bipolar disorder. During this hearing, Shipp admitted to misinforming investigators and that he, in fact, was primarily responsible for Slemmer's murder. He stated that he was drunk and tired and just wanted the police to leave him alone when he put the onus of blame on Pike. Additional testimony from prior Job Corps student and the defendants' mutual friend Tyrone Comfort stated that Shipp controlled and abused Pike despite her assertions that he was the first male to protect her and she admired the respect and fear he elicited from others. Pike, however, was heavily medicated during this hearing for her alleged bipolar condition and the hearing was rescheduled for April 2008.

During her 2008 hearing, prosecutors portrayed Pike as a cold-blooded vicious killer who not only planned Slemmer's murder but prolonged it for sport, essentially playing cat-and-mouse with Slemmer by allowing her to get up and try to escape and then pushing her back on the ground for additional torture. Ultimately, her request for a new trial was denied.

Pike became newsworthy again in 2012 when she formulated an escape plan with the help of 34-year-old New Jersey resident Donald Kohut who frequently visited Pike in prison but the extent of their relationship remains unknown, and 23-year-old former prison guard Justin Heflin. In a joint investigation by the Tennessee Department of Corrections, the Tennessee Bureau of Investigation, and the New Jersey State Police after receiving information about the plan, both men were arrested and charged with bribery and conspiracy to commit escape, with Heflin charged with an additional facilitation to commit escape charge due to his job as a prison guard. Authorities discovered contraband evidence in the facility which could have only been brought in by a staff member and that Heflin was likely involved. Further investigation demonstrated that Heflin knew Kohut and that Heflin was receiving gifts and money for his assistance in the escape plan. Pike was also charged.

Even more recently, during yet another post-conviction relief hearing in 2015, testimony revealed that Pike was allegedly pregnant at the time of the murder. While this may be true it neither excuses her actions nor provides any potential evidence of legal insanity to justify an affirmative defense of not guilty by reason of mental disease or defect or guilty but mentally ill. Also during this hearing, Slemmer's mother requested the missing piece of her daughter's skull so she could bury the whole of her daughter but was denied as the skull piece remains a critical piece of evidence in Pike's ongoing legal appeals.

Since exhausting the state appeal process, Pike's new defense attorney, Assistant Federal Defender Stephen A. Ferrell, filed a

123-page petition on her behalf alleging that he constitutional rights were violated in both the original 1996 trial and penalty phase and that Tennessee's appellate courts ignored said violations. Among these claims is that capital punishment would amount to cruel and unusual punishment in violation of the Eighth Amendment of the United States Constitution because of Pike's youth, immaturity and mental illness. While Shipp—only 17 at the time of the murder—was too young to warrant imposition of a death sentence, Pike was not. Ferrell alleged that her trial lawyers were incompetent and failed to introduce evidence of mental illness, brain injury, and post-traumatic stress disorder. In response, the state Attorney General submitted a 90-page rebuttal repeatedly asserting that the state courts' ruling were all legally correct. As of the beginning of 2016, this battle continues.

Numerous video interviews of Pike over the past several years show her admitting that she was fully cognizant of her actions and that they were wrong. She stated that she felt as though she was taking out years of abuse on Slemmer and that she committed a horrible atrocity and deserves to be punished; however, she asserts that she deserves life without the possibility of parole for her actions; not the death penalty for the actions of three individuals. She has repeatedly stated that she wishes it was she who died and not Slemmer but such protestations are moot after the fact. One cannot help but wonder if Pike actually means what she says or is simply saying what she thinks others want to her. Knoxville Police Department detective Randy York who worked the case has said that in his lengthy career he has not encountered many people who he believes are evil but that Pike is, indeed, the personification of evil and that she should never be permitted to be around other human beings ever again.

Experts assert that the death penalty is not an effective general deterrent and debate over the morality and legality of capital punishment remains contentious and in the forefront of public discourse and debate. Currently, Tennessee is only one of 38 states which have the death penalty. Whereas women comprise 13% of those arrested for murder, only 2% are sentenced to death and, of those, only 3% are actually executed; primarily due to judges not wanting to sentence women to death. In Tennessee, only two individuals on death row have been executed—both males. The last time a woman was executed in the state was in 1837. Many currently believe that Pike will likely never be executed.

SHE MATES, SHE KILLS: THE TRUE STORY OF TAUSHA MORTON

132

ALISON YALE

AN AGGRESSIVE FLIRT

Dewayne Barrentine met Tausha Morton in early 2007.

She worked as a teacher's assistant at his son's daycare. A single parent, Barrentine would pick up his son and would be greeted by Tausha on a daily basis.

"Whenever I would pick him up," Barrentine said. "She would always make sure to step out into the hallway and give him a hug and say 'hey' to me. She made herself very noticeable."

Tausha gave Barrentine all of the hints that she was interested. The sideways glance, the smile that lingered just a little too long. But still, he needed extra coaxing.

"One of her co-workers actually approached me," Barrentine recalled when a woman in the hallway had passed him a note.

"She said, 'It's a phone number,' I said, 'To who?' She said 'Miss Tausha and she wants you go give her a call tonight. And it started from there."

Smitten by the forward nature of the sweet-faced single mother, Barrentine fell hard.

The two began dating and began living together within a month.

"She was really there for my son...," Barrentine recalled. "I had full custody of him. He would lay in the bed next to me ... and I would hear him say his prayers and he would pray for a mama." He would soon feel the same way about Tausha's daughter, Lexie.

"We weren't dating even a month and she said, 'Will you be my daddy?' And I said, 'Baby, I'll be whatever you want me to be...'"

From that moment, Barrentine became hooked as Tausha made him feel as if she really loved him. She did all the little things from kind words to love letters.

He soon began to realize, however, that Tausha had a manipulative, lying nature.

The tall tales began to pile up. She told Barrentine that she had a "Bachelor's degree in Criminal Justice" as well as an inheritance due to her from an inhertiance.

"It was from her granddad who was a federal judge who was blinded by a battery blowing up in his face. If he was a federal judge, surely his name would be on docs under Google somewhere, but I never found anything."

Barrentine grew increasingly suspicious with Tausha's stories. He did some online investigating and discovered that she had a previous marriage with a man named Mitch Kemp. He confronted her about it and she would state that she had been married five times before.

The two vaguely resembled each other, big Southern boys, "teddy bears" that were more than a little overweight.

After eight months of co-habitation, Barrentine caught Tausha cheating on him.

He promptly threw her out of his home.

"I called the Sheriff's department," Barrentine recalled. "I was like, 'look, I don't care what y'all do with her, she's got to get her shit and get outta my house.'"

Wanting retribution of some sort, Barrentine accessed Tausha's MySpace account as he knew her password.

"Dewayne gets on her Myspace account basically to mess with her," prosecutor Richard Hicks said.

After sifting through her e-mails, Barrentine would make a shocking discovery.

"I found two or three e-mails," Barrentine said. "And they were from Mitch Kemp's sister-in-law."

Mischele Kemp had written Tausha an e-mail with the subject "We're really concerned."

"How is Mitch doing? We haven't heard from you in over our year? We would like to hear from you. If we don't hear from you immediately we will contact law enforcement and media. It is not like Mitch to disappear

for years on end without contacting his mother and we have became extremely concerned. Please contact us. We are very worried about him and your entire family. Sincerely, MK."

Digging a little deeper, Barrentine looked into Tausha's "sent message" box and it did not appear that she had ever responded.

"Immediately, I changed the password on the account," Barrentine said. "To where she couldn't access it and I printed off all those e-mails."

His actions would prove to be something bigger than a missing persons case. He would bring all of this information to the local police chief in Florida who instructed him to keep things to himself as he sorted things out with the Boone County Sheriff's Department in Missouri.

WHO WAS TAUSHA MORTON?

Tausha Morton, AKA Tausha Fields, met Mitch Kemp in 2001 when she lived in Colombia, Missouri.

Mitch worked as a carpet installer and had been recently divorced after fourteen years of marriage.

"It wasn't long after he got divorced that he met Tausha," Mitch's brother Rick said. "I would say within months."

Despite their eleven year age difference, Kemp fell hard for the young and vivacious Tausha.

Tausha was the proverbial "people person." Most of her friends and neighbors described her as someone who would make you welcome and treat you as if you were a long lost friend.

"She was bubbly," said one of Tausha's former employers. "Friendly and inquisitive. She paid attention and asked lots of questions about you."

Tausha liked learning about other people. She, in turn, would be all too willing to share details of her own struggles.

"She told us how her whole family was killed in a car accident," Rick Kemp said.

Tausha had a way of getting people to feel sorry for her. She would come across as a heavily burdened individual who suffered a lot of tragedy. People listening to her story would feel compassion for her lot in life and do what they could to help her.

Mitch Kemp listened intently to Tausha's tales of woe, buying them hook, line and sinker. He wanted to help her. To be her rescuer, her knight in shining armor.

The two began to date and by September of 2002, Tausha gave birth to a baby girl.

Mitch loved kids and was ecstatic. He proposed marriage and Tausha accepted.

"They got married in Pensacola," Rick said. "It was a very easy wedding."

The marriage seemed to look okay from all observers. Mitch's family didn't have any misgivings about Tausha, her charm enabling her to get into their good graces, at least at first.

"She was a really sweet girl," Carole Kemp said, recalling her first meeting with Tausha.

But over time, his family began to notice a personality change in Mitch. Sister Mischelle stated that he wasn't "as playful as he used to be."

Family gatherings would "take a back seat to things that she wanted to do" according to Tracy Kemp, who blamed Tausha's ability to manipulate.

As work responsibilities increased for Mitch, things began to go south in their marriage very fast.

DOMESTIC LIFE AIN'T FOR ME

Bored that she was left alone with the baby, the high-strung Tausha needed an outlet.

She would arrive at her friend's gym, the Body Zone, with her baby in tow. Soon she began working part time at the fitness center.

It was there that she would meet Greg Morton.

Morton was more physically fit than Kemp but he fit the same profile psychologically. He had recently broken up with a longtime girlfriend and was be vulnerable to the manipulative charms of Tausha.

"Greg was despondent over his break-up," a family friend said. "But when he met Tausha, he kinda perked back up."

Tausha used the same seductive strategy on Morton as she used on Kemp. She detailed her tragic back story. She told him stories of being molested, of being raped.

She also told Morton in no uncertain terms that her marriage with Kemp was on the outs. Making herself look like the victim, she told Morton that Kemp had made her miserable. He was abusive, bothered her constantly and threatened physical harm.

"She told him a bunch of lies," one of Tausha's friends said. "She said she was getting him (Mitch) served, that they were getting divorced."

By February 2004, her allegations of physical abuse would be reported to the police department as Tausha filed assault charges against him.

"She said he abused her," Rick Kemp said. "By assaulting her, or slapping her or something."

Tausha informed police that she and Mitch had gotten into an argument. Then he hauled off and hit her.

Mitch Kemp would plead guilty to the charges and spend over a month in jail. Upon his release, he would be in for another surprise.

Tausha had moved out of the family home and moved in with Greg Morton, taking Lexie with her. Morton had own a farm outside of Colombia, Missouri, a sizable estate that he inherited from his step-father.

A custody battle then ensued between Tausha and Mitch for their daughter. The fight would get uglier by the day with daily phone calls between the two and their attorneys. She would refuse to allow Mitch to see Lexie and used the courts to prevent visitation.

But Mitch Kemp would not give up without a fight.

"If he had to go through the court system to do it, he would do it," Mitch's brother Rick said. "But that he was going to see his daughter."

Tausha would state that their divorce was finalized in August as the custody battle lingered on. She would then marry Greg Morton the same month.

But Morton had no idea what he was getting into and a "triangle" domestic dispute ensued.

Tausha had arranged to meet with Mitch in order to get some personal belongings. She drove in with Greg to the house of Mitch's friend where he was staying. Mitch confronted Tausha on the front porch where he immediately berated her, screaming insults.

Greg was waiting in the car at the time and went to intervene on Tausha's behalf. Mitch became further enraged and hit Greg over the head with a patio chair.

Retreating, Greg and Tausha sprinted back to the car.

Mitch, however, would disappear after that confrontation.

THE DISAPPEARANCE OF MITCH KEMP

It took awhile for Mitch's disappearance to hit home for his family members and friends. He was the type of man whom you would not hear from from awhile but would suddenly show up on the front porch.

He was dutiful about calling his mother Carole and when she didn't hear from him, she began to worry.

"We called the Boone County Sheriff's office," Rick Kemp said. "About two weeks afterward, probably. We told them that Mitch had disappeared."

The Sheriff's department did not think any foul play was involved. They offered assurance to the family that Mitch "probably didn't want to be found."

Boone County detectives came to that conclusion after they found out that Mitch was wanted for stealing some goods from a friend. They believed he disappeared in order to escape from repercussions of his actions.

Meanwhile, Greg and Tausha were living large. In late 2004, Greg put up his farm for sale which surprised both his friends and family. He treasured the land as it was bequeathed to him from his stepfather. Those close to him believed that Tausha had put him up to it.

In February of 2005, the sale of the farm finalized. With a $275,000 payout in hand, he and Tausha left Missouri, telling no one.

The Kemp family continued to believe that Mitch was not missing and that Tausha was involved somehow. They just didn't have any evidence or clues. Just a damn strong suspicion.

"Something had either happened to Mitch that had nothing to do with Tausha," Rick Kemp said. "Or something happened to Mitch and Tausha had something to do with it."

Both the Kemp family and Boone County law enforcement would then find locating Tausha and Greg to be a fruitless exercise. They literally disappeared from the face of the earth, wanting a new life. Leaving no trail behind, Tausha and Greg would move all the way to the Gulf Coast.

Greg, still smitten by Tausha, would get a tattoo of her name on his back as if he were a branded cow. With a new man firmly under her control, Tausha would go on a spending spree which included getting breast implants with Greg's money.

NO SIGN OF MITCH

By February of 2008, the Kemp family still had not heard from Mitch.

"They took a missing persons report," Rick Kemp said. "But the case went cold, quite frankly, because they didn't do anything about it."

But the Kemp family would not give up hope. They continued their search, turning to the Internet to look for any trace of their beloved son and brother.

They would search different social networking sites and court systems to look for any trace of Mitch.

They found nothing for years.

Until Mischelle Kemp found Tausha on MySpace, the social networking account.

"My sister-in-law found an account," Rick Kemp said. "That had Tausha's name and picture on it."

Mischelle immediately sent Tausha an e-mail.

"Tausha didn't respond," Rick Kemp said. "But Dewayne Berrentine did."

REVENGE SEEKING BOYFRIEND TO THE RESCUE

Dewayne Berrentine read through Tausha's e-mails on MySpace and began connecting the dots.

"Her little stories," Berrentine said. "Just because somebody lies to me, that doesn't mean I'm going to call you out on it immediately. I thought that she was coming up with these stories to impress me, maybe?"

Dewayne had discovered that Tausha had gotten around. He received some disturbing information from a man that Tausha had dated after she met Greg and before she met Dewayne.

His name was Keith Jones.

"I was in love with her and anything else didn't matter," Jones recalled. "You couldn't verify anything that she said," he says. "You know, and I mean there were a lot of stories."

Keith and Dewayne exchanged notes and stories about Tausha. They realized that she told them the same outlandish stories. But then Jones told Dewayne a story that he didn't hear before.

He described how Tausha revealed to him that she was involved in the murder of one of her exes.

"She had a few drinks in her," Jones recalled. "She said this guy had raped her and her daughter. And she apparently ... went to where he was and lured him back to her house ... and he walked in the front door. And that's when Greg shot him in the chest."

Both men thought the story was "so far-fetched" and because of the lies they always heard from her, thought nothing of it.

Dewayne did eventually confront Tausha about the allegation and she dismissed it out of hand, saying that her ex-boyfriend would say anything to throw a wrench into her new relationship.

Dewayne would change his mind about things when he opened Mischelle Kemp's e-mail message to Tausha, however. After notifying the authorities, he also wrote Mischelle Kemp back who in turn contacted the authorities in Boone County. The Sheriff's department then reopened the case. After doing some sniffing around, they discovered that Mitch had "fallen off the face of the earth" and had not filed taxes in over four years.

Finally, the Boone County Sheriff department realized that something was wrong.

INVESTIGATING TAUSHA

Detectives decided to start researching the background of Tausha.

They would discover that Tausha's parents were alive contrary to her account that they were both dead. Mitch's mother had spoken to Tausha's father shortly before her soon was to be married.

"She said, 'Mitch, we need to talk,'" recalled Rick Kemp. "You've heard a bunch of stories. Her family wasn't killed in a car wreck. They're alive. They don't want anything to do with Tausha. They say she's nothing but trouble."

Mitch dismissed the notion of his mother. He was totally smitten with Tausha.

Further investigations would reveal that Tausha had been married and divorced twice by the time she met Mitch Kemp. She would go onto have four marriages before she was thirty and the number of men she lived were numerous. Mitch had no idea that Tausha went from one man to the next man to the next. Even if he did, he was so smitten by her early in their relationship that he would have probably ignored the red flags.

Investigators would further discover that her divorce to Kemp was never finalized so she may have married Greg Morton while she was still married to Kemp.

Tracking her movements after she moved from Missouri proved difficult. Tausha and Greg were eventually tracked to Alabama.

The couple lived an indulgent lifestyle, buying luxury homes and cars on the $275,000 sale they profited after selling the farm.

But it didn't take long for them to blow through the money.

Needing more income to support Tausha, Greg would go to Mississippi in the hopes of finding clean-up work after Hurricane Katrina hit. After he left, Tausha saw it as an opportunity to cut him loose.

She had to find someone new.

"While he was gone doing Katrina," Barrentine said. "She was blowing through his money. Then he came home finding another man laying in his bed and he's broke."

Greg would immediately file for divorce.

MEN AND MORE MEN

Cut off from her money supply from Greg, Tausha would find work as an assistant at a day care center. It was there that she would meet Dewayne Barrentine.

She would follow the same modus operandi in her seduction of Barrentine, telling him the sob stories of her life. She described how Greg Morton would abuse her and how she escaped. She gave details on how Greg would try to "jump on her" and that they had "several physical altercations."

Agreeing to let her move in, Dewayne would meet Greg when he was helping Tausha get her belongings out of his house.

The two didn't fight. Instead, they spoke briefly and Greg would later tell Dewayne about how detectives from Missouri were looking to speak with Tausha.

Barrentine would eventually discover Tausha cheating on him and throw her out of his home. She would find a new boyfriend a few days later by the name of Denver Workman.

Workman left his job and his extended family from Florida to Wilmington, Delaware after Tausha begged him to do so. Then she wanted him to move back and Workman refused.

"She would yell, scream and throw things at me because I wasn't leaving," Workman recalled. "She would tell Lexie I was a bad person and to kick me. I bought her a bus ticket to Florida and let her borrow my truck that was still down there. She took the truck, and I never saw her again."

Police would finally catch up to Tausha in Dothan, Alabama and confront her about the disappearance of Mitch Kemp.

During her initial interrogation, Tausha would firmly deny having any contact with Mitch.

"What do you mean what happened to Mitch?" Tausha would ask detectives in bewilderment. "I haven't had any contact with him. None."

The investigators continued to press, however, and Tausha would try to insinuate Greg as having something to do with Mitch's disappearance.

"They had words on the phone," Tausha told detectives. "And then they had, they got in a fist fight one time."

After being threatened with the possibility of being put in jail and leaving her five year old daughter Lexie in the hands of the state, Tausha then placed the blame on Greg.

"Greg killed Mitch," Tausha said. "He told me."

She would then inform detectives that she wasn't there when it happened. She stated that Greg left about 45 minutes later after he had yet another phone conversation with Mitch.

Tausha would claim that she feared for both her and her child's life because of Greg's temper.

She would recall that Greg shot Mitch on the farm. Investigators played along, even paying for her plane ticket to fly from Alabama to Missouri in order to let them know where Greg had buried Mitch. But once she arrived, Tausha seemed confused by the layout of the farm. She could not pinpoint where exactly the body had been buried.

She was then released under her own recognizance back to Alabama while Sheriff deputies proceeded to dig up the farm to no avail. They used ground penetrating radar, cadaver sniffing dogs but came up empty.

WHERE WAS GREG MORTON?

While talks with Tausha revealed some clues, investigators were even more eager to speak with Greg Morton.

After ending his marriage with Tausha, he settled in St. Louis. He was going to school to become an electrician and had a new girlfriend.

He wanted nothing further to do with Tausha. When investigators approached him, Greg immediately invoked his right to an attorney and refused to speak further.

Detectives did not have enough evidence to charge him. But they had Tausha on the run and spoke to her again. This go around, they decided to employ a little psychological manipulation.

"But I tell you what," Detective Dave Wilson said while sitting across from Tausha in the interrogation room. "He (Greg Morton) automatically assumed that you talked to us. Now, we didn't confirm that."

"Why did he think that?" Tausha asked.

"Well, there's only...who knows?"

"But he said he thought he'd talk to you?"

"I'm going to ask you again. Can you take us directly to where that hole was?"

This go around, Tausha said yes. The Boone County Sheriff's department flew her in from Alabama yet again to Greg Morton's farm.

This time, Tausha led investigators straight to where the body was buried.

Mitch Kemp's remains were dug up and his identity was confirmed.

"It didn't surprise us," Rick Kemp said. "But we were all just blown away. I mean, I just didn't want to believe that my brother was gone."

Investigators discovered that Mitch had been shot numerous times and found numerous shell casings in the makeshift grave. They then went to St. Louis and arrested Greg Morton.

"He wasn't surprised when we showed up," Detective Wilson recalled.

Tausha was allowed to return home but investigators had a suspicion that she was more involved than she let on.

A VOW OF SILENCE

Greg strangely refused to rat out Tausha, remaining in prison until he was officially charged.

Tausha moved to Texas, however, and began dating someone new. Investigators would catch up with her again, however, and this time a heated ninety-minute interrogation would ensue.

Their probing questions would force Tausha to change her story about Mitch's murder completely.

"I did not do anything," Tausha said after detectives informed her that she would be charged with first-degree murder. "I helped you in every way I could possibly fucking help you.

"Tausha," Detective Wilson said slowly. "We got people who say, say otherwise, okay."

Tausha then changed her story again, stating that she was present when Greg murdered Mitch.

"I snuck around behind Greg's back and I saw Mitch, okay," Tausha said. "Greg had no idea."

She stated Greg would kill Mitch in a jealous rage after they returned from a hotel for a tryst. They then drove back to the farm and Greg assaulted Mitch before he got out of the car.

"He had a gun in his hands," Tausha said. "It was a black gun. Mitch started walking backwards. I ran inside the house and then I ran back outside. I saw that Mitch was walking backwards, and Greg was walking towards him. And Greg shot him. I didn't kill Mitch. I didn't want Mitch to die."

But the investigators didn't see it that way. They charged her with first-degree murder.

THE TRIAL

In June of 2009, Tausha had been imprisoned for over six months as she awaited trial.

Her bail was set at one million dollars.

Greg Morton then decided it was time to cut a deal. He broke his silence on what really happened the day of Mitch Kemp's murder. He would admit to his involvement in exchange for a more lenient sentence if he testified against Tausha.

In 2010, Tausha's trial began.

The prosecution's argument was that Tausha was the mastermind behind the murder, that even though Greg pulled the trigger it was Tausha that put the idea in his head. They also believed that Tausha's motive was to have sole custody of their daughter.

The defense would claim that Tausha was innocent and the victim. Her attorney was, in essence, using the same technique that Tausha used on all of her men. They would play on sympathy and hope that the jury would be as charmed by Tausha as all of her men.

GREG MORTON CONFESSES

Morton would take the stand and tell the jury exactly how Tausha manipulated him to kill Mitch.

"She's hysterical," Morton recalled. "She said Mitch raped her."

"What are you feeling, Greg, at this point?" Prosecutor Hicks asked.

"I wanted retribution. Tausha took charge and handed me a gun the net morning. She goes, 'I'm going to get Mitch, and when I get back, you shoot him.'"

"What were you going to do, Greg?"

"I was going to do what she asked me to do."

"They made a plan in that Tausha was going to go in town and pick Mitch up," Rick Kemp said. "And tell him that Greg was out of town."

Mitch arrived at the farm, thinking that it would only be the two of them. But then Greg emerged from the porch.

"I had a gun in my hand," Morton recalled. "I raised it and pointed it at him. I kinda paused I was kinda struggling with it a little bit. And then she started yelling at me to shoot him."

Greg believed that he was committing a protective act. He believed that Mitch was raping Tausha and molesting their six-year-old daughter.

"Then she said 'You got to get something to move him. Get something to move him with.' Greg recalled. "Then she said, 'Come on. You should have had this ready.'"

"And you saw that she was still struggling?"

"He was."

"So what did you do?"

"I shot him again."

"Was he struggling anymore?"

"It was over," Morton said. "I used farm equipment to pick up Mitch's body and we buried him in a pit. When we were rolling the dirty on Mitch she said 'Mitch Kemp is a piece of shit and nobody is going to look for him for a long time.'"

The defense would then call a neighbor who testified on Tausha's behalf, stating that she thought she was under Greg's control.

Greg then broke down on the stand and tearfully apologized to Mitch Kemp's family.

Over time, however, he began to realize that Tausha was a cunning liar. As he got to know her better, he realized that he had been duped.

"He'd been played like a fiddle by her," Rick Kemp said. "She did it to every man that she had."

Tausha was not called to the stand by the defense and the jury would find her guilty.

"I think she thought she was going to walk," Rick Kemp said. "She thought she could just get away with lying and manipulating people."

Tausha Morton was sentenced to life in prison without parole but is currently appealing her sentencing.